THE MONTESI SCANDAL

Karen Pinkus

THE MONTESI SCANDAL

The Death of Wilma Montesi

and the Birth of the Paparazzi

in Fellini's Rome

The University of Chicago Press • Chicago and London

Karen Pinkus is associate professor of Italian, French, and comparative literature at the University of Southern California, where she also chairs the Department of French and Italian. She is the author of *Picturing Silence: Emblem,
Language, Counter-Reformation Materiality* and *Bodily Regimes: Italian Advertising under Fascism.*

The University of Chicago Press, Chicago 60637

The University of Chicago Press, Ltd. London

© 2003 by Karen Pinkus

All rights reserved. Published 2003

Printed in China

12 11 10 09 08 07 06 05 04 03   1 2 3 4 5

ISBN: 0-226-66848-7 (cloth)

Library of Congress Cataloging-in-Publication Data

Pinkus, Karen.

The Montesi scandal : the death of Wilma Montesi and the birth of the paparazzi in Fellini's Rome / Karen Pinkus.

    p. cm.

ISBN 0-226-66848-7 (cloth : alk. paper) — ISBN 0-226-66849-5 (pbk. : alk. paper)

1. Montesi, Wilma. 2. Italy—Politics and government—1945–1976. 3. Italy—Social conditions. 4. Paparazzi—
Italy. I. Title.

DG577 .P52 2003

945.092'5—dc21

                         2002152762

This book is printed on acid-free paper.

THE FOLLOWING IS BASED ON A TRUE STORY, HOWEVER IMPLAUSIBLE IT MAY SEEM. ALL OF THE NAMES, FACTS, DATES, TIMES, AND EVENTS HAVE BEEN UNCHANGED AND EVEN DOCUMENTED (TO THE BEST OF THE AUTHOR'S ABILITY) IN ORDER TO PROTECT THE CINEMATIC ASPIRATIONS OF THE CHARACTERS INVOLVED.

CONTENTS

CAST OF CHARACTERS

The Montesi Family

WILMA MONTESI   Twenty-one-year-old "Anygirl" from Rome. Engaged to a police officer who is stationed in a provincial town.

WANDA MONTESI   Wilma's sister, several years older.

MARIA PETTI MONTESI   The mother. Is she a bossy, bitchy matriarch prone to fits and cursing in public, or a submissive housewife?

RODOLFO MONTESI   The father. Hardworking proprietor of a woodshop, still handsome, although prematurely aged by the scandal.

SERGIO MONTESI   Wilma's younger brother, a schoolboy.

ZIO GIUSEPPE   Zio means uncle in Italian, and all Italy knew of Giuseppe Montesi, brother of Rodolfo, uncle of Wilma, Wanda, and Sergio, simply by the name "Zio Giuseppe." A dashing accountant with a car, Zio Giuseppe lived with another one of Rodolfo's siblings, Ida Montesi. In all, there were ten children of Wilma's grandfather Riccardo Montesi.

Key Figures in the Case

ADRIANA BISACCIA   A rather plain young woman from a small town near Naples, she moved to Rome with dreams of becoming an actress. Worked as a typist for Silvano Muto's gossip sheet (see below).

ANNA MARIA MONETA CAGLIO "The daughter of the century," a vivacious young woman from an old-money, Milanese family. Came to Rome to make it in the movies and ended up having an affair with Ugo Montagna (see below).

AMINTORE FANFANI Left-wing Christian Democrat and chief political rival of conservative Attilio Piccioni. How far would he go to gain power?

ANGELO GIULIANI Wilma Montesi's one-time fiancé. The couple met in a Roman dance hall and had only a few real dates. Not a rocket scientist.

FABRIZIO MENGHINI Former lawyer, journalist for the gossipy daily paper *Il messaggero di Roma*. Later retained as advisor to the Montesi family.

UGO MONTAGNA Brash entrepreneur of Sicilian heritage. Lover of Anna Maria Caglio. Friend of the rich and powerful, he managed a private hunting reserve near Rome. Known for hosting "decadent" parties.

SILVANO MUTO Law student and aspiring journalist who started a tabloid gossip magazine in the early 1950s.

TOMMASO PAVONE Chief of Italian police. Friend of musician Piero "Morgan" Piccioni (see below).

PIERO PICCIONI Jazz musician and composer, in art "Piero Morgan" (a name that sounded American, perhaps almost black). Studied law to appease his father, Attilio Piccioni, one of Italy's most powerful politicians and a high-ranking member of the ruling Christian Democrat Party. Piero was often spotted with celebrities and jet-setters. Dated actress Alida Valli.

SAVERIO POLITO Chief of Rome police. Friend of fellow-Sicilian Ugo Montagna.

MARIO SCELBA Right-wing Christian Democrat, minister of the Interior in 1953, and thus ultimately responsible for activities of both Rome and Italian police chiefs.

RAFFAELE SEPE Obese magistrate of the Roman courts.

MARIELLA AND ROSSANA SPISSU Two sisters who lived in a shack on the outskirts of Rome. Mariella was the "official fiancée" of Zio Giuseppe for over twelve years; Rossana carried on an affair with Zio Giuseppe and bore his child.

ALIDA VALLI The starlet. Queen of the Fascist melodramas known as "white telephone" films. Also known for many later roles, including a suspect widow in Hitchcock's *Paradine Case*.

In *La dolce vita,* Emma (Yvonne Furneaux) slumps against a wall after a (failed) suicide attempt. Although she is alone within the narrative of the film, her character appears hyper-aware of the presence of the camera.

PROLOGUE

Credits roll over (mostly female) suicides. Women jumping from faded marble bridges into the Tiber River in the center of Rome. Scene from Federico Fellini's *White Sheik* (1952). The young newlywed Wanda holds her nose and plunges into the shallow sludge of the river, fearing that her groom might wrongfully suspect her of being anything other than "pure and innocent." Fellini's choice of the name Wanda for his protagonist may be significant. The name sounds vaguely exotic, as if it should belong to a gypsy, perhaps signifying, for Fellini, escape from the gray boredom of Fascist control. Fellini's Wanda wears a sequined costume, and her dive suggests the performative nature of any gesture of self-annihilation. Scene from Michelangelo Antonioni's "Suicide Attempt" episode of the cinema-verité "news magazine" produced by Cesare Zavattini, *Love in the City* (1953), in which a woman reenacts her attempt to drown in the Tiber with great dispassion. Women throwing themselves from third-floor windows of sixteenth-century buildings. A woman cautiously downs a vial of sleeping pills and fluffs her pillow before climbing into bed. Film clip of Emma's attempted suicide from Fellini's *La dolce vita* (1960) followed by aftermath of Steiner's successful suicide from the same film.

This is not, strictly speaking, a work of academic theory. Nor is it journalism. It is, rather, a series of notes of various registers and intensities for an unrealized screenplay. These notes tell the story of an *actual* scandal that took place in 1950s Italy, but the narrative is often interrupted with asides, cultural details, and critique concerning primarily the intersections of cinema, paparazzo photography, tabloids, femininity, and politics.

The form of an unrealized screenplay is by design. The Montesi case cannot be comprehended outside of a conceptual framework of the cinematization of everyday life that took form in postwar Italy. To be more specific, there are two axioms to consider before we plunge into the details of the narrative: This case is fatally imbricated in the cinematic, and this film remains impossible. I will certainly address concerns that have been central to cultural studies, literary, and film theory in recent years. In fact, the very idea of everyday life makes of this unrealizable film a potential object of philosophical analysis in the tradition of Henri Lefebvre, Michel de Certeau, and the school of "everyday life" that sprang up as a theoretical construct in the postwar period in France and in the wake of the institutionalization of American cultural hegemony. This story will expand on the relationship between the quotidian and the cinematic analogy, for while this relationship is discussed frequently in a broad sense, few writers have radically immersed themselves in its minutiae. The case is profoundly like a film.

Shot of Ennio Flaiano, Fellini's collaborator on *La dolce vita* and many other projects, sitting in a café on the Via Veneto and speaking aloud the words he writes in his journal: "Is another reality at all necessary? Is this rosy Roman reality not sufficient? Certainly, it is hard to live and be judged in a city where the one industry is cinema. One ends up believing that life is a function of the cinema, one becomes the photographic eye, one sees reality as a reflection of what lives and palpitates on the screen."

We must not fail to mention in the same breath as cinema the origin of paparazzo photography, the production of vernacular imagery in which stars and ordinary people come increasingly to resemble one another. Fellini and Flaiano coined "Paparazzo" (a Calabrian character from an obscure Gissing novel; perhaps acoustically related to an obscure word in dialect for an annoying insect buzz) as the proper name of the character of a photojournalist in *La dolce vita*. Paparazzo accompanies Marcello (Marcello Mastroianni) as he reports on various events and scandals on the Via Veneto and around Rome. Fellini and Flaiano based the character, in part, on Tazio Secchiaroli, a photographer who honed his signature style by photographing two of the protagonists in this narrative, as we will see. The connections between a certain style of still image, cinema, and scandal are profound. For instance, *La dolce vita* owes much to the Montesi scandal. But it is more difficult to grasp the ways in which this scandal might not have erupted had a new style of filmmaking not emerged in Italy in the wake of neorealism—a new style that seemed to mobilize the paparazzo shot, with all of its contradictions and instability.

The subjects of the paparazzo shot, like the subjects of this unrealizable film, are captured in the interstitial moments of daily life, as they pull their collars around their faces, as they climb awkwardly in and out of cars or slip on sunglasses, posing as if they did not want to be seen, and yet unknowable as subjects beyond the flash of the bulb. What will come to define the paparazzo shot at its base? Is it the compositional resistance to being snapped, or "taken"? A class spectacle in which the (working-stiff) photographer attempts to gain access to the rich and famous for the purpose of ridicule? Is it an actual method or style of shooting? Or is it a series of narrative elements (chase, avoidance, capture) that came to be most profoundly realized in the version of Princess Diana's death that blames photographers on scooters for the car crash? Mohamed Al Fayed, Harrods' owner and father of Diana's boyfriend Dodi, insisted on reopening proceedings against the photographers who trailed the famous couple. The photographers, acquitted of manslaughter, have now been convicted of breaking privacy laws in France by taking pictures of the dying pair. Does the law of a democracy that promises "respect for private life" extend to the interior of a car? Is the very notion of "private life" knowable outside of the technologies and practices of the photographer?

To begin to answer these questions, we turn to Italy of the 1950s, for although examples of "candid" photography certainly predate this period, the modern paparazzo shot crystallizes in Rome around the time of our screenplay. First: the matter of cars. A number of Italian cars from the early fifties, including the immensely popular Fiat 600 driven by various protagonists in this story, had doors that opened from front to back, leaving the driver (or passenger) relatively vulnerable to the onslaught of photojournalists. The entire front panel of the peculiar Isetta "microcar," released in 1953, served as a door for the driver and possibly one passenger. Driving in an Isetta, the human body is folded into itself like a germinating seed in a pod, utterly exposed as it unfurls. The paparazzi themselves often rode on scooters, the emblematic mobile transport unit of the Italian economic boom. Motor scooters (which were often built with two seats, perfect for a driver and a photographer) allowed the paparazzi to negotiate traffic and to take open shots without the constrictions of car windows and doors, and this mode has endured. Politicians, actors, singers, and foreign nobility drove themselves around the city, along predictable routes. They parked on the street. I am not the first to point out that Rome of the 1950s and early 1960s was an ideal place for this coincidence of eager photographers and quasi-reluctant celebrities. Wealthy visitors stayed in one of only a handful of deluxe hotels, all located near the center of the city. They frequented nightclubs like Victor Bar or the Rupe Tarpea (where Anna Magnani slugged a photographer in 1955). They drank exotic cocktails and danced the mambo. Barriers of privacy that demand telephoto lenses and that have become increasingly common in recent years were not yet necessary, and that is why the early paparazzo shots are not as grainy as some of the more scandalous or even quasi-pornographic shots published in today's tabloids. Photographers mingled with their subjects, as street life was especially porous. In fact, "porous" was a term used by both Walter Benjamin in his essay on the primitive social economy of Naples and by Siegfried Kracauer in his highly influential book *Theory of Film: The Redemption of Physical Reality* to describe the permeability of Italians before the camera. These two German critics found in Italians a kind of natural photogenic ingenuousness.

It is Thursday, April 9, 1953. Wilma Montesi, a middle-class girl of twenty-one from Rome, spends the morning tidying up the apartment she shares with her parents, sister, brother, and maternal grandparents. Close-up of Wilma's hand—with nails painted bright red—as she dusts a photograph of herself in a silver frame—a headshot that will soon become an icon. It is important that we never really see an establishing shot of Wilma, only point-of-view shots of the apartment, with occasional pans over to the window and into the large courtyard of Via Tagliamento number 76, lush with foliage—palm trees, mimosas, fragrant oleander. Goldfish swim in a shallow marble pond. Laundry hangs from lines strung outside the windows. The building dates from the 1920s and isn't far from Termini, the central train station of Rome. It was originally intended to house railroad workers, but for some years now it has been a middle-class building.

The specter of female mobility in the city haunts this case. *Termini* is the terminal point for optimistic Italian girls coming to Rome; and then leaving Rome when they are spent. It is the point where Italian subjects become accountable for their provincial origins, or can be located by a democratic form of state surveillance. It is also a civic space where beggars congregate, where unsavory characters are escorted by police and put on trains to other places with writs of obligatory deportation. It is, in fact, characteristic of the period in question that the police exploit various atavistic forms of control, remnants of the not-so-distant Fascist past. As our story is set in Rome, we should keep in mind the de facto mutual dependency of the national police force and the civic police (the quaestor) in the city. Both forces, staffed by men of ex-privilege who continue to operate along embedded lines of conduct while invoking a new rhetoric of democracy, are under the aegis of the Ministry of the Interior. From their centrifugal, *terminal* point of power they enjoy the right to exile citizens to the provincial towns and peripheral cities of an Italy that is still overwhelmingly rural. Citizenship in the new democracy cannot be revoked, but *residency* in the capital is provisional.

Wilma's uncle, Zio Giuseppe, is trapped by reporters as he climbs out of his Fiat 600.

Claretta Piccioni, sister of musician Piero Piccioni, is caught by reporters as she gets of a car during the Montesi trial.

A model demonstrates the 1953 Isetta microcar, "the smallest four-wheel vehicle."

The first paparazzo, Tazio Secchiaroli, drives an associate, Luciano Mellace, on a Lambretta. The picture was taken in 1952, one year before Wilma's death, during an anti-American rally in Rome. The photographers managed to capture the police making an arrest, and the image of the Lambretta, with the police in the background, was published in the left-wing *Evening Country*, a newspaper that will figure in our own screenplay.

Wilma Montesi is just finishing her menstrual period. She places her sanitary napkin belt and slightly bloodied panties in the sink to soak. She puts on a fresh pair of underwear. Such details may strike the viewer as gratuitous and intrusive. Only later will we learn the importance of these intimate hygienic practices. Wilma walks over to a dresser in the dining room. The camera pulls back to reveal two extremely narrow beds, one on each side of a long wooden table. This is where Wilma sleeps alongside her older sister, Wanda. The carpentry is fine yet functional. Most of the furniture was made by Wilma's father, Rodolfo Montesi, a carpenter who runs his own modest workshop in the neighborhood. This furniture is not "contemporary" (a designation of midcentury style in architecture and design identified with picture windows, bright fabrics, playful lamps; and streamlined kitchen "workstations" for the "modern bride") nor is it strictly infused with nostalgic values. The Montesi furniture embodies the banality of the expenditure of middle-class labor, something approaching a hypothetical middle-class utopia of self-sufficiency that remains tauntingly elusive as Italy finds itself approaching the threshold of the boom of consumer culture.

A careful pan across these rooms will serve to define, for our viewers, the tastes of the postwar Italian *ceti medi*—the middle classes: the artisans, small shop owners, and white-collar workers in cities and towns. These individuals will contribute to and benefit from the economic miracle later in the decade. For now, though, they are slowly growing in numbers as peasants abandon rural poverty for regular wages and regular hours in the city.

It is 2:00 P.M. The Montesi family has just finished lunch: a potato purée, bread, and apples. Wilma and Wanda clear the table. Their father, Rodolfo, hurries back to work at his woodshop. Their mother, Maria Petti (women in Italy often keep their maiden names after they are married, a gesture, one might say, that places them in a double bind between father and husband), looks through the newspaper for a matinee. She suggests Jean Renoir's *Golden Coach*, which is showing at a local cinema, but Wilma doesn't like the star, Anna Magnani, who seems too brash, too overtly theatrical, too vulgar. As a reader of tabloids, Wilma would have been aware of her steamy affair with Roberto Rossellini in the late 1940s. The couple kept a love nest on the Amalfi coast. Prone to fits of jealousy, Magnani once threw a shoe at Rossellini's face after he flirted with a Miss America. Several years before our screenplay begins, Rossellini offered the lead in *Stromboli*, originally written for Magnani, to Ingrid Bergman. On a nearby island, the scorned and passionate Mag-

Anna Magnani in *The Golden Coach* (1953). "Where does theater end and life begin?"

nani filmed *Vulcano*. All of this boiling volcanic activity would have offended the sensibility of a placid girl like Wilma Montesi.

"Where does theater end and life begin?" asks Anna Magnani's commedia dell'arte–inspired character in *The Golden Coach*. Almost as if in response, Wilma notes, "That isn't a very nice film." Nevertheless, Wanda and Maria Petti put on lipstick and prepare to leave.

Some time later. Close-up of Wilma's hand as she takes her house keys from a box on top of her dresser. We see that she deliberately leaves behind her gold bracelet, a tiny gold necklace, and a pair of pearl earrings.

Our film will bring to the surface a series of material objects that constitute female ephemera: bracelets, garter belts, postcards, diaries, snapshot photographs, and so on. We should not assume that such items are either disposable or unworthy of our full attention.

PART ONE
Wilma Goes Out

The prologue is easy. Before our film begins, Wilma Montesi is an Anygirl—*una ragazza qualunque*, in Italian. She speaks the type of ordinary language that Henri Lefebvre understood as the very referent of everyday life. This language is the flattened, affectless prose of Anygirls, like the young artist's model in Alberto Moravia's 1960 novel *Boredom*.

Moravia's Cecilia speaks with "brevity and impersonality." The novel's protagonist notes: "It seemed as if in her mouth words lost any real significance and were reduced to abstract sounds, as if they were spoken in a foreign language that I did not understand. The lack of any dialect or social inflection, the complete absence of any revealing clichés, the reduction of all conversation to pure and simple statements of incontrovertible fact like 'It's hot today,' confirmed this impression of abstraction."

An Italian advertisement from the period reads, "A girl without stockings is an Anygirl." (*Una ragazza senza calze è una ragazza qualunque*: shortly, we will see the irony in showing this ad for our particular narrative.) Perhaps the camera can pass this advertisement (in an English translation) plastered on a billboard as Wilma Montesi crosses Via Tagliamento. We will not be troubled to find ads written in English. So many films made during the 1950s and 1960s and set in Italy feature Italians who just happen to speak fluent English: the "tour guides" in *Three Coins in the Fountain*, David Lean's *Summertime*, or *Roman Holiday*, released the year our screenplay begins. In the 1958 Technicolor melodrama *Seven Hills of Rome*, American TV singer Marc (Mario Lanza) asks Raffaela (Marisa Allasio, the "Italian Jayne Mansfield") how she comes to speak English so well. "During the war," she stutters. "The Americans wanted us to."

In our screenplay, it is cinema itself that serves this universalizing function. Our translator is the Hollywood™ brand. There is a kind of linguistic-cinematic colonialism that begins to develop during this period, and we might acknowledge this movement ironically by showing a poster-hanger, like Antonio Ricci of *The Bicycle Thief*, plastering over an Italian version of the *"ragazza qualunque"* ad with an English version. Shot of Antonio Ricci putting up poster of Rita Hayworth from the movie *Gilda* just before his bicycle is stolen.

But to call Wilma a *ragazza qualunque* is also to situate her everydayness in a particular political dimension at this time in Italian culture. Wilma must at any cost be preserved as a plain and ordinary girl of no particular importance, no particular sexual fascination. The adjective *qualunque* and its neologistical, nominal form, *qualunquismo*, also refer to the extraparty political position of the bourgeoisie in the post-Fascist era, the

Antonio Ricci hanging poster in *The Bicycle Thief* (1948).

"noncommittal man" whose opportunism gave space to the rhythmic fluctuations of Right and Left that do not preclude one another, but rather, oppose themselves to the extremes of antidemocracy. Anyman Party founder Guglielmo Giannini, who had once embraced Mussolini in order to have a career in film, described the *uomo qualunque* in the following terms: "He was the man in the café, at the cinema, in the bedroom, in the dining room, at the tax bureau: Everywhere. His rights are indisputable, even if powerful minorities threaten to cancel them out. He is someone who contrasts himself with the hero, the leader, the king, the *duce*, the führer, the conductor, with Churchill, with Roosevelt, with Stalin. 'What do I care about your affairs?' says Anyman. 'I want to live freely without being bothered by anyone and above all, without being involved in your polemics." The party slogan was Don't break our balls.

If we were to see Wilma, she would appear as if through a filtered lens, in soft tones of black and white, like Anygirl of the Italian postneorealist or "rosy neorealist" cinema. This label refers to films (in black and white) like *Bread, Love, and Fantasy* made after the twenty-odd "genuine" and committed neorealist films by directors such as Rossellini and De Sica. The term "rosy" refers, then, not to the literal introduction of colorization of the film stock but to a slackening of mood. Cinematic daily life has been rendered more palatable.

In the late 1940s, the leader of the "Anyman" movement, Guglielmo Giannini, sponsored protectionist legislation decreeing that at least twenty *Italian* films had to be shown per quadrimester in Italian movie houses. And at the same time, Christian Democrat leader Giulio Andreotti became undersecretary to the prime minister and passed another law forbidding export of any film that portrayed Italy in a negative light. After this, it became politically and financially expedient to film real life with a rosy lens. Stars such as Sophia Loren, Gina Lollobrigida, Silvana Mangano, and others emerged from Anygirlness into the rose-tinted spotlight after winning beauty pageants. Nothing would stand in the way of a Wilma Montesi proposing herself (perhaps against her parents' will) as Miss Rome, except the vague suggestion of immorality associated with the public display of the female body.

We must not see Wilma Montesi. To film her in full would be to grant her "Anygirlness" a specificity that she does not merit. And when she does achieve iconic status—after her death—she is supposed to be the subject of a film called *Wilma Montesi*, starring the members of her family; a film that would bear her name, but in which she would not appear, except as symbolic presence. No film was made. But this does not diminish the idea that cinema implodes into everyday life.

◯

As Wilma leaves her building, we should find some way—perhaps through a series of
fade-ins and -outs—to indicate the departure from this very building, indeed, from
the same stairwell, several years earlier, of Anna Maria Pierangeli. Raised by ultra-
strict Catholic parents, Anna Maria was three years older than Wilma (and one year
older than Wilma's sister, Wanda Montesi). She is discovered in Rome by producers and offered a contract by MGM. In Hollywood, she will change her name to
Pier Angeli and fall in love with James Dean. Her mother forbids her to see the
rebel actor and virtually forces her into a marriage with Italian-American Vic Damone. She becomes pregnant and arranges a meeting to inform Dean. Two days
later he is killed in a car crash. Pier Angeli's marriage is a tragic farce. She tries to
flee with her child to Italy, reconciles with Damone, and then later they are divorced. She becomes involved with Italian composer and band leader Armando
Trovaioli, the mentor of a young musician named Piero Piccioni (more later about
him). In the early seventies, facing her fortieth birthday, with a history of bad films,
and still pining for Dean, Pier Angeli will OD fatally on barbiturates in Beverly
Hills. In her time, Pier Angeli serves the conservative Christian Democrats in Italy
as a model for all that is wrong with Hollywood and America; she also serves young
Roman girls as a model for all that they might hope for, now that the war is over,
now that prosperity is just around the corner. "Pier Angeli" never returns to live at
Via Tagliamento 76, but she remains a powerful symbol through her absence.

◯

The camera leaves the Montesi apartment with Wilma, crossing the large, deserted
courtyard of Via Tagliamento 76, moving quickly through the entranceway, paus-
ing nervously to acknowledge the doorkeeper, a middle-aged woman perched on a
stool, underneath a clock that reads 5:20. We do not know if the clock is accurate,
or even if it is running since there is no second hand.

**As we film the movement from the building to the street from Wilma's point of view, we
should consider the imperative to represent Rome as a peculiar space, built on layers
of history. Wilma's neighborhood is composed of buildings, not on the model of the ancient *domus*, or freestanding private house, but rather the *insula*, or "block," subdivided
into flats or *cenaculae*. The innovation of the *insula* was its verticality. It developed in
response to the exceptionally rapid population growth in ancient Rome. The floors of**

the *insula* were organized around a courtyard, and the city developed many regulations to keep them from going too high, as they were prone to collapse. Avaricious owners, who often lived in ground-floor apartments, tried to get away with ever taller buildings. Each era of Roman history witnessed taller *insulae.* In humbler *insulae,* the ground floor was divided into stores or *tabernae.* Each *taberna* opened onto the street with folding wooden shutters that could be closed and bolted at night. These are the predecessors of the modern metal roll-down shutters in Italy that tend to grant street-level businesses a generic, sterile front during off-hours. While it would be implausible to have a voice-over lesson in Roman domestic architecture during Wilma's walk down the street, we must find a way to indicate the ancient origins of the modern apartment complex, and all of the urban problems that are embedded in its history: code evasions, cramped quarters, high rents, security issues, landlord-tenant disputes, and, above all, problems of human waste disposal. While Wilma Montesi is decidedly unaware of any such history, her ignorance could be, precisely, representable in our film. The exit from the stairwell, across the courtyard, the passage through the arched doorway, past shops with their shutters rolled down halfway, perhaps past a Roman fountain spouting pure water—these movements must be filmed to demonstrate Wilma's willful disinterest in the past, and they make her a modern girl.

Until now Wilma has been an Anygirl, but now we must begin to make certain choices that will cause aspects of her to come into focus, her edges to sharpen. We don't really notice that Wilma is wearing a short yellow wool skirt with green dots, and a tufted jacket. Whatever shots we may imagine of Wilma are not glamour shots. The camera may pan down and catch a glimpse of her stocky but shapely legs, in nylons, and her black antelope shoes with green trimming and gold buckles (it was precisely these shoes, according to Wanda, that caused Wilma's blisters, leading her to use iodine, and subsequently, to need a footbath. Later we will appreciate the importance of the point-of-view shot of the shoes). We follow Wilma onto the street (or rather, we follow her legs), and we lose her as she turns the corner.

In Alberto Lattuada's episode for the multidirected "investigative film magazine" *Love in the City* (1953), a camera follows girls' legs as they parade around Rome in the springtime. Repetitive twangs from a Jew's harp punctuate the soundtrack. The episode contains only a very slight narrative: at the end, the camera moves away from its peculiar point of view, calf-high, and pans up to follow a man who follows a girl's legs onto a tram. The tram rolls on, until it finally grinds to a stop at the *capolinea,* on the periphery of Rome. The woman's legs disappear around the corner of a melancholy,

In Alberto Lattuada's episode for the multi-directed "investigative film magazine" *Love in the City* (1953), the camera takes on the point of view of a man following a girl's legs all the way onto a tram. The tram stops at the *capolinea* on the periphery of Rome. The legs disappear into the doorway of a melancholy, characterless postwar housing project, crossing an invisible border before which the man, and the camera, find themselves suddenly halted. The ground floor of the building includes a series of doorways, like the old Roman *tavernae*, with metal shutters. It isn't clear if these doorways are stores that are already closed for the evening, or empty spaces that have yet to be filled by prospective businesses.

characterless postwar housing project, crossing an invisible border before which the man and the camera find themselves suddenly halted. It is evening, and we have wasted time. We must catch the tram and get back to the center before dark. Tomorrow we start again, watching legs.

It is now 8:00 P.M. Maria Petti, Wanda, Wilma's father, Rodolfo, and the youngest Montesi—Wilma's brother Sergio—all arrive home and cross the courtyard of the building together. Rodolfo carries groceries in a sack; Sergio, a satchel filled with his schoolbooks. Maria Petti glances up toward the window of the family's apartment, expecting to catch Wilma gazing out as she often does when left alone.

Approximately 30 minutes later. Still wearing a light overcoat, Maria Petti hurries back across the courtyard to the small office in the building's entranceway. She nervously asks the doorkeeper, "Did you happen to see Wilma go out?" The clock now reads 8:30. The doorkeeper reflects for a moment and responds. Yes . . . Wilma did go out, alone, at . . . around 5. No, to be more precise . . . between 5:15 and 5:30. Let's say 5:20. How can she be certain? A group of men have been patching the building's tin roof. They always finish at 5, then pause to wash their hands, talk, linger. The workers had left the premises at 5:10. The doorkeeper, Signora Roscini, recalls looking at the clock as they filed out. Not more than ten minutes later, Wilma went out. It must have been around 5:20. (The doorkeeper never budged from her account. Not after years of prodding). "At least she was alone," Maria Petti notes. "I was afraid they might have taken her." Signora Roscini nods her head in sympathy, as if she intuitively understands what Maria Petti means by "they." Years later, Roscini will also be able to recall that Wilma left without her jewelry. From her perch under the building's portico she manages to survey the distilled minutiae of everyday life, not out of boredom, but because it is her function to do so.

Maria Petti and Rodolfo stand in the entranceway. It is now 8:55 P.M. on the office clock. Rodolfo weakly tries to reassure his wife as he heads off for the tram to the Tiber River. He will search for Wilma around the bridges. Perhaps his daughter jumped. That's what they do in the movies. That's what one reads in the papers. He'll also try the morgue. Tearfully, Maria Petti begs to use the office phone. She dials her in-laws. Rodolfo's parents live with several of their grown children in a crowded apartment on the other side of the city. Maria Petti appears particularly interested in reaching Rodolfo's youngest brother, Giuseppe Montesi (later to be known simply as Zio—uncle—Giuseppe), who owns a car, a miniature Fiat 600 station wagon with wood trim. A car would help in the search for Wilma. But Maria

Petti learns he is not at home. Rodolfo's sister, Ida Montesi (Rodolfo is one of ten children—we should keep in mind that large families received prizes during the Fascist era as well as considerable financial benefits), promises to hurry over. Maria Petti hangs up. "I was hoping my brother-in-law . . . with his car . . . ," she trails off as the doorkeeper switches off the lights and closes the large iron gates to the main entrance. "I'm closing up now," says the doorkeeper. Choking back tears, Maria Petti scurries across the courtyard to the apartment. Maybe Wilma has called in the last few minutes.

At 11:30 P.M. Rodolfo reluctantly files a missing person's report with the district police.

In *The Bicycle Thief* Antonio Ricci files a report on his missing bicycle before an utterly distracted officer. A bored reporter with notepad sticks his head into the room and asks, "Anything?" "Nothing," replies the officer. "Just a bicycle." The scene is a powerful one for the ethics of neorealism. The theft of a bike wouldn't even merit mention on the fourth page of the paper, the page of *cronaca* or human interest stories, even though Ricci's livelihood depends on it. In Fellini's *White Sheik* Ivan files a missing person's report on his new bride Wanda. At least this situation might demand a few lines of text. The chronicle of Wilma Montesi does begin on the fourth page, but after a time it will move to the first, as a young reporter named Fabrizio Menghini moves with it. The character of Marcello in *La dolce vita* is a *cronista*. Fellini actually knew Menghini and may have based Marcello on him. Moreover, Fellini's cowriter, Ennio Flaiano, worked a stint at Menghini's paper, the *Messenger of Rome*. In its historical context, the *cronaca* emerged as a journalistic strategy for resisting the lingering tinges of Fascism. The first official item of *cronaca* actually appeared as early as 1944 when the Fascist police chief of Rome was tried in the high court of justice and was subjected to a public lynching in the papers. From its first appearance in Rome, the *cronaca* proceeded north with the Allies, and its journalists, far from finding themselves marginalized, often moved to top positions in their respective papers. In this sense, the *cronaca* is not merely synonymous with gossip or with human interest, but with exposures of scandal and corruption, with moral outrage, and with the naturalism of everyday life.

7:30 A.M., *Saturday, April 11.* It is a windy, overcast morning. Wilma's body is discovered exactly thirty-seven hours and fifty minutes after her disappearance, by a sixteen-year-old construction worker who is riding his bike past a deserted beach outside of Rome. There can be little doubt that Fellini had Wilma's body and its aftereffects in mind when he conceived of the final scene of *La dolce vita*: stunned jet-setters on the morning after a drunken striptease/orgy view a monstrous fish

In *The Bicycle Thief,* Antonio Ricci combs the banks of the Tiber River for his son Bruno after hearing that a young boy may have drowned. Bruno, it turns out, has simply moved from the spot where his father left him.

Antonio Ricci files a report on his missing bicycle in *The Bicycle Thief*. A bored *cronista* inquires whether there is anything of importance. "No," replies a policeman. "Just a bicycle."

washed up by the high tide. Fellini asked his designer, Gherardi, to fabricate something simultaneously plausible and excessive. The director refused to see the object until the day of shooting, so that he himself would be surprised. Gherardi kept deferring its construction. Finally he fabricated a sort of ray with convex lenses for eyes that exaggerate their size. In the film, the partiers can't decide whether to take the horrendous fish home or throw it back. Its glassy eyes stare upwards as it portends of a putrid future.

A small crowd begins to gather around Wilma's corpse, which is dressed in gloves, sweater, a yellow tufted jacket fastened with one button at the neck. Her skirt is hoisted around her waist and we can see that she is missing her shoes, stockings and garter belt. She wears simple white cotton panties decorated with teddy bears. The camera may not get close enough to the body to establish that the panties are decorated with teddy bears, since there was some debate about whether or not these were actually *her* panties. She lies face down in the sand with her feet toward the sea; some of the onlookers decide to drag her ever so slightly up to drier ground.

It isn't until late in the evening that the attorney general's office finally imparts the order to remove the body. A medical examiner and several policemen from the carabiniere force (the rough equivalent of the French gendarmes, an independent, highly selective branch of the military), dressed in stiff blue uniforms, lift the body into a waiting ambulance. We follow the ambulance as it struggles across the sand to the semipaved coastal road. "They're taking the Burma Road," says a local as the ambulance pulls away. There are few houses near the beach, and no establishments aside from a boarded-up cabana. This is a private beach, and unpopulated in April save for a few locals. Separating the road and the beach is a strip—about thirty feet wide—of lush Mediterranean vegetation. Trailing the ambulance is a journalist, perhaps in a convertible sports car like Marcello of *La dolce vita* in his Triumph.

The journalist presents himself at the door of a tiny coroner's office in the town of Pratica del Mare ("knowledge of the sea"). At first he is shooed away by the attending officer, but he then shows his business card.

"I was asked to oversee the examination," says the journalist, coughing nervously.

"Ah," says the officer. "A lawyer. We thought you were a journalist."

"No, no," says the journalist. "A lawyer. I was asked . . ."

The journalist, a big-boned, extremely tall man, is ushered into the office and begins to take notes on a tiny pad. Shot of the photographer who waits in the car outside, chain-smoking filterless Camels.

There can be little doubt that Fellini had Wilma's body and its aftereffects in mind when he conceived of the final scene of *La dolce vita*. Stunned jet-setters on the morning after a striptease/orgy view a monstrous fish washed up by the high tide.

The local coroner, Dr. Di Giorgio, is amazed at the state of perfect preservation of the corpse. He notices sand in the girl's underpants. When he lifts the eyelids, Dr. Di Giorgio observes that her pupils are rigid, a state that occurs approximately twelve hours after death. Based on a compromise between the pupils and the more extreme rigidity of the fingers and toes, the doctor estimates death had taken place eighteen hours earlier—that is, sometime on April 10. Without knowing anything of her circumstances, Di Giorgio leaves open the possibility that the dead girl spent the night of April 9 away from home, alive, somewhere. He notes that the cause of death was certainly drowning.

The article announcing the discovery of Wilma's body in the Roman daily, the *Messenger*, is extraordinarily long for an item of *cronaca*. Why? Is it because, as the unsigned article notes, her corpse is both "beautiful and unidentified"? The article gives such a minutely detailed description of the girl's hair and eyes, her clothing, and the state of her corpse that immediately Wilma's death seems larger than Everyday Life.

The Rome city morgue, Sunday, April 12. Rodolfo Montesi has gone to identify the body of his daughter, along with her fiancé, a police officer named Angelo Giuliani who has been stationed for several months away from Rome, in the small town of Potenza. Rodolfo takes one look at the corpse and slumps in a chair. As attendants revive him, Giuliani breathes deeply and proceeds to make the identification, mumbling either: "They took her from me" ("*me l'hanno uccisa*") or else "they took her" ("*l'hanno uccisa*"). A subtle distinction, but not without importance as we will learn later. In any case, we are unable to make out his exact words. The first expression would imply a passion that, by all accounts, appeared lacking in Giuliani's relation with the dead girl. (In testimony at the Venice trial Giuliani never denies making a similar expression, but claims he meant nothing in particular by it as he was simply overwhelmed by the site of a large bruise on Wilma's face.)

Once the identification is complete, two doctors perform an autopsy. Based on the results, they place the time of death at approximately 7:30 P.M. on the night of April 9, several hours after Wilma's disappearance. In this, they depart from the findings of the coroner who first examined the corpse, Dr. Di Giorgio. However, they concur that the immediate cause of Wilma's death was drowning. They find no traces of any illicit substances in Wilma's stomach, and so they do not bother to check her spinal cord or brain. They also find Wilma to be in a state of "integrity" (within a certain margin of error intrinsic to such investigations), although they note certain red abrasions around her vagina, leaving open the remote possibility of sexual activity. The doctors find traces of almond and milk in Wilma's stomach and they theorize that she had consumed a gelato before going into the water. We might represent the medical examiners' version of the death in rather rosy tones, as a flashback, with a soundtrack of an innocent pop song: the beach; a close-up of a postcard signed "Wilma" with a heart dotting the *i*; an ice cream.

POV shot up from corpse as medical examiners poke and prod it. We will overhear one doctor speaking (perhaps with a deliberately distorted voice to emulate the auditory POV of the deceased Wilma Montesi), "So you see that refrigeration does not completely stop the decomposition process."

The afternoon of April 14. Stating the identity of the "beautiful dead girl," the late edition of the *Messenger* publishes the Montesis' exact address—not only the street, but even the stairwell and apartment number, along with a headshot of the victim that will come to be reproduced literally thousands of times, to the point that it loses its representational status and is transformed into a pure and exemplary simulacrum.

Given these published details, it would be a simple matter to look up the Montesis' number in the Rome phone book. Rosa Passarelli, a heavyset woman who works at the Department of Defense, does just that. She telephones the apartment on Via Tagliamento and says that she has information about the case that she would like to discuss with the family. Although Rodolfo has gone with Zio Giuseppe, Angelo Giuliani, and Sergio to the seaside to question possible witnesses, two police officers in civilian dress are present at the Montesi apartment when Passarelli calls. The police urge Maria Petti not to divulge their identity, but instead to refer to them as relatives.

Rosa Passarelli arrives promptly, explaining that she recognized the girl in the newspaper photograph as the same one with whom she had shared a compartment on the 5:30 P.M. train to Ostia on April 9. Ostia, the name of the old Roman port city, has a public beach with a tiny train station that is overflowing in summer. Wilma, let us recall, was not found at Ostia, but at a private beach, a good distance away. Passarelli, a "university woman," as we will be constantly reminded, is not fooled by the police officers in spite of their attempts to pass as relatives. She offers a minutely accurate description of Wilma's clothing and demeanor on the train. She says she was particularly struck by the girl's black and green antelope shoes (which had not been described in the press, since Wilma was found without them). Wanda and Maria Petti listen with rapt attention to Passarelli's words, including her assertion

Courtyard of Wilma's building with an arrow indicating her apartment.

ATTORNO AL "CASO" MONTESI

that on the train to Ostia, Wilma appeared absolutely calm, and showed no sign that she was about to fling herself into the ocean. Passarelli is even able to offer information about the girl's undergarments, which she had been able to glimpse through Wilma's slightly opened legs. (On the other hand, Wanda will testify that Wilma nearly always sat with her legs tightly crossed.)

The Montesi women appear to be entranced by Passarelli's classy demeanor, her accuracy, and her compassionate, maternal mode of speaking. So Wilma went to Ostia after all! She could have taken the train from the San Paolo station. God knows how. She didn't know Rome's public transport system. (The conversation excludes the possibility that a young woman, communicating in her native tongue, might be capable of asking directions if she didn't know the train route.)

Maria Petti begins immediately to confide in Passarelli, explaining that Wilma was terribly timid and never went out alone, and that the family was pleased for this reason that she had gotten engaged, "even if it wasn't a particularly good marriage; not a very desirable marriage, considering how beautiful she was." In turn, Passarelli comforts Maria Petti, saying, "Why do you want to exclude the possibility of an accident?" (In Italian, a *disgrazia*.) Yes, Maria Petti agrees, it must have been accident! The woman is "heavensent." The idea of this woman of letters glancing between the thighs of Wilma as the train lurched along is comforting. Even Wanda appears to Passarelli to soften as the witness helps the family replace suicide with the theory that Wilma must have traveled, alone, to Ostia, in order to bathe her feet of the unsightly iodine stains that appeared after the girl had attempted to soothe the calluses caused by her new antelope shoes. Of course! Hadn't Wilma been begging to take a footbath for the last several weeks? And wouldn't Ostia be the most likely place for her to go wading? She must have made up her mind to make the trip all by herself, perhaps as a way of asserting her independence. She went to the water's edge and began to wade. Perhaps she was struck by a sudden fainting spell or cramp and she fell, unconscious, into the ankle-deep water. There was the small matter that her body was not found at Ostia (where the train terminates), but rather, twenty kilometers to the south. On the other hand, if a high-class "university woman" like Passarelli saw her on the Ostia train, she must have drowned there!

Wanda should appear bossy at this point, urging, "Yes! An accident! Let's say it that way from now on." Rosa Passarelli continues drinking tea and keeps the grieving Montesi women company with thoughtful interventions and apparently genuine concern. But by this time the two police officers have grown bored and have politely excused themselves so there are no witnesses to the solidification of the footbath theory. In any case, Passarelli later relates that she had the impression the theory had been "fried and refried" (to translate an Italian idiom literally) even before her arrival in the house on April 14.

The word "footbath" (*pediluvio*) becomes part of Everyday Life. We might show this by filming stern parents warning their adolescent girls to avoid seaside footbaths. Look what befell Wilma Montesi! A cinema magazine called *Black and White* features a cartoon showing the "pediluvio universale" a pun on the "deluvio universale," the biblical flood.

Was Rosa Passarelli really "heavensent" or was she dispatched to the Montesi household by more earthly forces? What was she doing on the 5:30 train to Ostia (if she really was on the train)? Passarelli says she was going to Ostia to visit a friend, a certain Signora Bassignani. As soon as the two women met up, "for some silly reason," Passarelli went on about how she saw a particularly beautiful girl on the train wearing a spongy yellow-green jacket, but without any jewelry or other ornaments. Why did Passarelli bother to tell her friend about Wilma, and how is it that she happened to note so many details? Signora Bassignani recalls asking Passarelli, "What are you, fixated on this girl?"

Most fortuitously, the two friends happen to be together again, several days later. They are having coffee and reading the paper, when Passarelli comes across the description of Wilma Montesi and exclaims, "My God, that's the girl from my compartment on the train!" Passarelli, along with various other witnesses who will claim to have seen Wilma at Ostia on the afternoon of April 9, agree that she was much more striking than the descriptions, and even more beautiful than her photographs. Unfortunately, all of the other Ostia witnesses will later disappear, be discredited, or end up recanting their own testimonies.

About a month after Wilma's death, "university woman" Rosa Passarelli buys an expensive apartment in the center of Rome. Is this pure coincidence, or has she suddenly come into a large sum of money related to her visit to the Montesi family?

And if Wilma did travel on the 5:30 train to Ostia, when did she leave her apartment? Shots of police attempting to reach the train station by various means. Police assess the absolute minimum times for the trip from Via Tagliamento to the San Paolo station as follows: eighteen minutes in a car; an hour and a quarter on foot; fifty minutes running; and twenty-four minutes with the fastest tram, without traffic, and assuming the tram arrived immediately at the stop nearest to Wilma's apartment

University woman Rosa Passarelli "before" and "after" she realizes she is being photographed.

building. Given the unwavering testimony of the Via Tagliamento 76 doorkeeper—that Wilma left at 5:20—it would have been impossible for Wilma to make the same train as Rosa Passarelli. If we believe the doorkeeper (not a "university woman" but a self-confessed "tough customer"), then Passarelli could not have seen Wilma. If we believe Passarelli, we must discredit the doorkeeper. Whether Passarelli deliberately lied or was merely mistaken about the girl in her train compartment, she had certainly planted the suggestion that if the Montesi family went along with her version of the story, they could only help the family name and the future prospects of Wanda, in particular.

Rosa Passarelli pretends to shun the spotlight of the cinematic gaze. But there is a place on film even for the Passarellis of this world. For now we must recall that Rosa Passarelli of the Ministry of Defense offers the most concrete support for the notion that Wilma went alone to Ostia, for a footbath.

Friday, April 17. A week after Wilma's disappearance the case is officially solved and is set to be "archived," pending receipt of the medical reports and completion of all paperwork. Police put forth two plausible hypotheses, each with its own logical intricacy:

1. Suicide. But Wilma had not shown any apparent signs of depression—after all, she was engaged to be married and sent her fiancé cheerful postcards, whose contents she also dutifully copied into a notebook. And why would she have taken her house keys, or meticulously washed her undergarments that very morning, or removed her garter belt at the beach, if she meant to take her life? (Police determined the force of the tide was not enough to remove it—no easy task, as one medical expert testified, nostalgically recalling his adolescent training in this area. In fact, the sea, although rough, had not been strong enough to remove Wilma's little jacket fastened by only one button near the collar). And why go all the way to Ostia, or even to the private beach at Tor Vaianica, where she was actually found, when the Tiber River, right in the heart of the city, had well served many young girls determined to take their lives?

2. Drowning by "misfortune" (*disgrazia*). But how could a healthy young woman drown in ankle-deep water? And if Wilma had merely gone to bathe her feet, then again, why remove the entire garter? Why not simply unclip the stockings? Finally, if this footbath and drowning did take place in Ostia, how did the corpse end up approximately twenty kilometers away in Tor Vaianica?

Finally, police cannot fully rule out homicide. Someone—a "brute" as the *cronaca* liked to say—may have dumped the body at the beach. It is possible that Wilma was still alive, but unconscious at that time. In any case, the final cause of death was, unequivocally, drowning.

Various shots of groups of Romans reading papers at bars and discussing Wilma Montesi's death.

Later that day. During a tearful ceremony, Wilma is buried in her nearly finished wedding gown. Based on the extensive press coverage, and the portrayal of Wilma as a "good girl" who met with misfortune, young women who never knew Wilma attend the funeral in a show of support. In a brief period, Wilma Montesi has become a public figure, a martyr-heroine for all young girls struggling to better their status in life and yet maintain some sense of moral dignity. Wilma's headshot is hung on her tomb in a silver frame, and the accompanying inscription reads:

> Died April 9, 1953 [Actually, this is the day of her disappearance, not necessarily the day she died]. Pure creature of rare beauty, the sea at Ostia carried you away to leave you on the beach at Tor Vaianica—it seemed as though you slept the sleep of God, beautiful as an angel. Your mother, your father, your sister and your brother are near you in their great love and immense suffering.

During the procession through the cemetery Zio Giuseppe insistently asks a journalist named Doddoli about the progress of the police investigation.

"Why are you so concerned?" Doddoli asks aggressively. "Did you have something to do with it?"

"Please. Leave me out of it," Zio Giuseppe begs. The scene must be ambiguous, as is the emotional intensity of Zio Giuseppe's response.

April 20. Three days after the funeral, the *Messenger* publishes an unsigned article titled "In the Margins of the Tragic End of the Young Wilma Montesi." Later, we will learn that the *cronista* following the case for this paper is actually Fabrizio Menghini, the same individual who presented himself as a lawyer in order to observe the initial inspection of the body at Pratica del Mare. This explains how the *Messenger* had been able to provide a detailed description of the body and implicate itself in the family's identification. The article suggests that while journalists (including the author himself) have responsibly (and "democratically"!) reported on the facts given them by police spokesmen, the average man on the street be-

WILMA GOES OUT

Wilma's tomb adorned with the famous headshot.

lieves that the case was closed much too swiftly. All of Rome talks of the exquisite corpse on the beach, and no one is convinced by either the suicide or the *disgrazia* theory.

Shots of various groups of Romans discussing the case.

Then, unexpectedly, on April 22, journalists are granted a meeting with the chief of the "flying squad," the branch of civil police initially in charge of the investigation, formed after the war by a politician named Mario Scelba. Scelba has recently been promoted to minister of the Interior and he oversees all of the police. A Christian Democrat, he is to the far right on the political spectrum. He is also friendly with rich and famous individuals, including a dapper Sicilian hunting preserve manager, as we will see later. Let us note, for now, that it was Scelba's "flying squad" that dismissed the possibility of homicide and declared the death accidental.

Shot of police announcing results of their investigation as reporters eagerly take notes:

On April 9, Wilma Montesi of Via Tagliamento 76, suffering from calluses caused by her new antelope shoes, left her apartment and headed to the San Paolo train station. Although her family claimed she had no knowledge of public transport, it is certainly plausible that she had access to the information necessary to cross town. She boarded a train to Ostia, intending to bathe her feet. She arrived at Plinius, the largest public beach nearest to the Ostia train station where several witnesses had already claimed to see her at a café (and we must recall that Wilma's picture had been published in the papers on April 14). Finding the area a bit too crowded for her liking, the modest girl decided to move up to the next beach at Castel Fusano where, believing herself alone, she removed her shoes, stockings, and even her garter, in order to wade, unimpeded, in the water. Wilma could not swim. She was struck by a sudden illness—probably due to her postmenstrual state—and she drowned. Someone later came and removed her clothes from the beach. Castel Fusano is close to a deep canal into which Wilma's body must have floated. The body was then carried a fair distance south to Tor Vaianica where it drifted toward shore and lodged in the sand.

To some degree, the whole case at this point hinges on the question of the garter belt. Wilma's father gives detailed testimony, noting that his daughter always wore a simple, 20 cm long band of black silk around her waist. As it moved toward the back, the band diminished in size until it was about the width of the elastic itself—6 cm. On the left side there were 5 fasteners. Wilma only wore the garter when she went out. She did all the fasteners for fear the garter might slip off. Our viewers may be struck by the

intimate knowledge Wilma's father seems to possess about his daughter's garter. At other points in our film, however, he will appear detached, out of touch with Wilma's desires. A former maid contradicts Rodolfo, noting that Wilma actually wore a one-piece bra-girdle-suspender belt, fastened so tightly that the maid had to help her put it on and take it off. Clearly, a full-piece would be removed by the tide only with the utmost difficulty, and not without dragging off the victim's shirt or sweater. On the other hand, one might understand that Wilma would remove such a restrictive garment (were she actually wearing it) in order to enjoy greater freedom of movement on the beach. Wanda testifies that her sister would never have taken off her suspender belt on a public beach unless she felt so sick that she absolutely had to—in extremely hot weather, for example. Who can legitimately speak to the particulars of Wilma's undergarments, her peculiar habits, her tics? Her father seems to have the last word, like a stern voice-over dubbed over an ambiguous scene in a narrative film, but should his authority over her most prosaic manners be questioned?

As Fabrizio Menghini notes in his unsigned piece in the *Messenger*, the police version of events has not convinced the public. The paper has already begun to receive many letters from all over the country, including one that states: "A man opened the gate of the old royal hunting reserve (Castel Porziano) for a car which had entered the other gate at Capracotta [*sic*—this means "cooked goat"; as we will soon learn, the estate in question is actually called Capocotta, "cooked head"] with a man and a woman on board. The person who observed this may even know the name of the driver, and has recognized the dead woman in the photographs published in the papers as the very passenger in that car."

As we will learn, a car did indeed pass through the reserve around the time of Wilma's death, exiting a gate not more than two kilometers from where Wilma's body was discovered, and then parking on the dirt road along the beach. The passengers got out and "spent some time together," as the papers euphemistically reported. The driver of the car will turn out to be Prince Maurizio d'Assia (Hesse, in English), nephew of the last king of Italy. Could he have been involved with Wilma? For a few days, members of the press hint at scandal and search for clues to support their suspicions. There is, however, no evidence to link the prince with Wilma's death.

Capocotta had long been a royal hunting ground, retooled in the postwar era as a private club for wealthy gentlemen. A vestige of the monarchy, Capocotta posed uncomfortable questions for the democracy. It was a sort of no-man's-land, neither private property nor land with free public access. Stocked with game like the lavish reserves of Renaissance princes, Capocotta was a potential target for critics who delighted in accusing the ruling class of profiting from antiquated forms of social connection. To enter this magical terrain, one had to be invited, and most important, it gave access to the sea. Surrounded by fences and protected by tall trees, Capocotta was a breeding ground for ambivalence and paranoia in the developing democracy. To this day, it has retained something of its regal aura: it is the property of the Italian president.

○

Under pressure from the press and the public, the police agree to conduct a second "informal" investigation (i.e. without involving the judiciary, since no criminal act is suspected) into Wilma's death. This second investigation will last for months, and will reach the same conclusion as the first.

○

The son of a powerful right-wing politician named Attilio Piccioni sues two journalists from a left-wing newspaper, *Evening Country*, for implying he may have been involved in the death of Wilma Montesi. It is too early in our story to furnish details about this matter, or even to name the politician's son, so we might choose to film a brief snippet of the settlement. We will hear the journalists formally agree to retract everything they reported. They will also consent to donate fifty thousand lire to the House of Fraternal Love, the politician's favorite charitable organization, in lieu of compensatory payment to the (still unnamed) victim of slander. During this scene, the camera should linger on the defense lawyer, Giuseppe Sotgiu, establishing his features for the viewer. We will have occasion to film him later in a rather piquant context. After the settlement, the defendants thank Sotgiu and call him "Comrade."
In the next shot we see the politician's son, toasting with friends in a busy nightclub.

○

Shot of Julius and Ethel Rosenberg being strapped into their electric chairs in Sing Sing.

○

Roman holidays. August 1953. A series of political maneuvers that may strike the viewer as irrelevant and highly uncinematic, but they are nevertheless crucial to the plot of

La dolce vita's Signora Steiner returns home to find a throng of photojournalists, some from the left-wing *Evening Country*. Unaware that her husband has committed suicide after murdering their two children, Signora Steiner asks, "What? Have you mistaken me for a movie star?"

our screenplay. Italy's president, Luigi Einaudi, selects a leader of the Christian Democrats by the name of Attilio Piccioni as De Gasperi's successor for prime minister. Piccioni is considered the most stable, moderate member of the party, a man with a reputation for coalition-building. Respected by the nationalistic and patriotic Right, as a former member of the Populist Party, Attilio is also free of any overt links to the Fascists. Piccioni does not even have a phone in his house so he does not learn he's been selected until parliamentary leaders knock on his door. We could film the party arrive, make their announcement, and then, looking slightly hung over, we see Piccioni's son emerge from a back room. "What is it, Papa?" he asks.

"I've been named . . ." We now notice that the son is the same individual who, in the previous scene, had settled a lawsuit with the two journalists.

Meanwhile, the elderly De Gasperi decides to leave Rome for a brief vacation in his hometown in the mountains near the Austrian border. As he boards a train, a journalist asks what advice the former prime minister would give to Piccioni. "Let me cite from Proverbs 35," lectures De Gasperi. "Do not deviate toward the Right or toward the Left" [sic]. The train wheels begin to churn, and De Gasperi fades in the distance. Finally, after a great deal of collective research, journalists locate the citation, in Proverbs 27. Ironically, in the Bible, the phrase is followed by a verse that the former prime minister leaves off, either consciously or unconsciously. This second verse of Proverbs 27 reads: "Avoid the path of evil; the Lord loves those roads which lead to the right, but those on the left are dangerous."

Although the threat of a vote of no confidence will prevent Attilio Piccioni from reaching the highest office, he is transformed during this period into a figure of great moral authority.

September 1953. Summer is drawing to a close and Italians begin returning home from the beach. A promising young law student named Silvano Muto has pieced together modest funds to launch a new tabloid magazine called *Actuality.*

Attualità, which literally translates as "current events," is a key term for our screenplay, and one that deserves further investigation. What is meant by "current events" in the age of the "serious democratic newspaper," the *cronaca*, and the tabloids? First, we must note that actualities were one of the earliest forms of cinematic production, in the late nineteenth century. Newsreel-style documentaries of stars and other novelties dominated the film catalogs. Many of these actualities were "arrival" and "departure" films of trains, thus making the term a key one for our own screenplay, which hinges, in part, around the plausibility of just such a brief train journey. Second, in the context

of the 1950s, when actualities had long been replaced by feature-length films, actual time was not reducible to "the present" for a number of reasons. Italians tried to live time in the early 1950s as discontinuous with the time of Fascism. The ruling parties attempted a series of purges and ruptures. The Mussolinian calendar that began re-counting time in marble-etched Roman numerals with the founding of the regime— November 5, 1921—was recanted, and normative time restored, even if some of the pristine monuments could not be rechiseled. The late 1940s inaugurated a period of refoundings. A great deal remained at stake in actuality, which did not begin at any precise point, but was characterized by a break from the past.

In a famous essay titled "An Aesthetics of Reality" from *What Is Cinema?* André Bazin wrote that Italian cinema should be viewed as unique in its concern for *actual* time, even when the subject of a given film is not contemporary life. For Bazin, Italian films appeared above all as "reconstituted reportage," exhibiting a "natural adherence to ac-tuality," which makes Italian national cinema a form of radical humanism.

Actuality was specifically linked in the postwar period to the rhythm of information in weekly magazines. It was not up-to-the-minute time like live television, which was not yet established in Italy. Indeed, Italian television, offering only one channel, had not yet learned to exploit and engage with everyday life, and the presenters and commen-tators appeared artificially stiff. Weekly tabloids were, in turn, bound up with cinema. If cinematic time was actual, this did not refer, precisely, to the time-image repre-sented within particular scenes of a film or to the forward motion of scrolling in the projector. These would be more formal questions that would interest film theorists. Nor can actuality in cinema be reduced to the history lessons of newsreels (which have essentially disappeared since the war). Rather, it is related to the tempos of re-portage surrounding the making of a film and the ways public interest is raised in con-junction with the release of a picture. In other words, although the time lag between the shooting of the film and its release is relatively long, the reportage and photogra-phy around the film make it appear fresh, and the actors must inhabit a kind of actu-ality that bridges that gap.

Actuality allows for a peculiar temporality existing between the "first and unique in-stance" of an event, and a certain repetition or stagedness. In *La dolce vita* the pa-parazzi demand that movie star Sylvia (Anita Ekberg) return to her plane in order to exit a second time. Viewers immediately understand that this repetition is no less au-thentic than the first time. Indeed, Sylvia's second appearance may be the genuine event—prepared by the dress rehearsal that precedes it.

In *La dolce vita,* paparazzi demand that Sylvia (Anita Ekberg) return to her plane in order to exit a second time. Viewers immediately understand that this repetition is no less authentic than the first time.

Flash photography develops around an aesthetics of perpetual night. In many of the zinc or rotogravure prints from the period, objects have a reflective sheen to suggest a kind of hypertime, like time in the casinos of Las Vegas. It is not accidental, for example, that many of the paparazzi, including Tazio Secchiaroli, began their careers as young *scattini*, itinerant photographers who snapped pictures of soldiers and tourists in Rome, hoping to capture their imagination and capitalize on their desire for souvenirs.

In the immediate postwar period, the *scattini* were funded by larger studios, so they would offer their customers cards with the location where they could pick up their pictures if they wanted to purchase them. Or they would pretend to take pictures, trying to gauge the customer's level of interest—this activity flourished prior to the explosion of tourist cameras. There was, then, a notable risk involved in the snapping: most tourists didn't bother to visit the studio, so the *scattinis'* labor went unpaid. *Scattino* photography implies a low snapping to printing ratio. The studios only printed up the images they managed to sell, but the photographers, like Secchiaroli, focused on the interactions with their subjects, and on the charades involved with the shooting itself, rather than on technique, printing, or distribution of the images. They learned English phrases to coax a sale out of a customer. They engaged in bartering and other tactics. It is thus essential to stress the temporal and ideological disjuncture between the act of snapping, and the final production of the image. As the cultural memory of the war begins to fade, many of the young photographers attach themselves to photo agencies. As proto-paparazzi, they transfer their skills to a new activity—shooting stars or people of note. They retain their mobility, and their images reflect a peculiar, tense relationship between photographer and subject, a temporal game where, at the very least, one can say that the subjects do not pose before a neutral camera, but engage in some form of banter with the shooters, who themselves gain notoriety. This interaction, retained in the published image, is emblematic of actualized photographic time (as opposed to the timelessness of a studio shot of a prepped and dressed glamorous star).

The cover story of the first issue of Silvano Muto's scandal sheet, *Actuality*, is "The Truth About the Death of Wilma Montesi." It isn't that the public has forgotten Wilma—her name would still be recognizable to most Romans—but the case isn't fresh, and so this headline achieves a certain shock value that helps *Actuality* stand out on the overcrowded newsstands. Shot of Muto reading aloud his version of events in a bohemian café:

Wilma, like so many other innocent, middle-class girls, was seduced into a world of "existentialists" and "cinema people." Perhaps she sneaked out when her parents were not paying attention; perhaps they lived in a state of denial; perhaps they were lying to police about their daughter's habits in order to preserve her good name. Like it or not, the girl was known to have attended a drug and orgy party at a hunting preserve outside of Rome, managed by a certain Signor X, an ambitious former member of Mussolini's secret police, and frequented by a certain Signor Y, the son of a prominent Christian Democrat minister. After snorting cocaine provided by Signor Y, Wilma passed out, possibly because she was not used to the drug (possibly because, as we learn later, her heart appeared particularly small). Signor Y, believing her dead, drove through the preserve and exited the gate onto the beachfront road. [We should recall that gossip earlier circulated about Prince Maurizio d'Assia enjoying the "royal privilege" of the private beach road.]

According to Muto, Signor Y dumped Wilma's body on the shore in order to make the death seem like a drowning. In reality, she was only unconscious and she actually died in the water. Signor X, the manager of the estate, could be considered an accessory in that he helped arrange for the body to be transported. There had probably been a cover-up. Police evidence had been tainted by certain figures in power. So says *Actuality*.

Shot of Nadia from *La dolce vita* at her divorce party/striptease whispering through a hole in the side of a tall wicker chair, "private love-making insults me!"

Journalist Silvano Muto is immediately questioned, but police dismiss his article as unfounded trash. About a month after the publication, Muto appears before a magistrate and sheepishly admits he made the whole thing up. He gets a slap on the wrist and continues to publish his tabloid on a shoestring. That might have been the end of the story . . .

We should indicate a sense of potential filmic closure with a long shot of Muto walking off into a crowd at sunset. In a short time, we will be forced to radically disrupt this finale.

However. That same month—*September 1953*—several colleagues of Wilma's uncle, Zio Giuseppe, approach journalist Fabrizio Menghini at the elegant *Messenger* offices near the base of Via Veneto. "We have some things to tell you about Giuseppe Montesi," say the workers from the printing plant where Giuseppe does bookkeeping several afternoons a week in order to supplement his income from his regular job with the state. "Giuseppe is a suspicious type. He receives phone calls at work from women. He once boasted of owning a bachelor flat in Ostia. Girls ring him. He once said that there was nothing wrong with having feelings for one's niece as long as she was worth it. He claimed he was going to pay for a certain girl's wedding dress on the condition that she would sacrifice her virginity to him in an act of *ius primae noctae*. . . ."

Menghini takes notes.

And finally the printing plant workers get to the heart of the matter: "On Thursday, April 9, Giuseppe received a phone call at about 5:00, approximately thirty minutes after he arrived at the plant. He asked to be excused because he had to go to Ostia to meet someone. We countered that it was not a good time to leave since the following day was payday and it was Giuseppe who prepared the checks. He begged us to cover for him. . . ."

We will see Fabrizio Menghini reacting coolly to all of this, as a good *cronista* should.

Shot of Marcello from *La dolce vita* in sunglasses reacting coolly as a Via Veneto source whispers gossip in his ear.

"Why are you coming to *me?*" Menghini asks, "And why are you only coming forward *now?*"

Biagetti, who manages the printing plant, speaks for the others. "We feel that the investigation is taking a wrong turn. Heads may roll and it isn't fair. We have nothing personal against Giuseppe Montesi, but if heads are going to roll . . ."

In the next sequence of shots we see the four printing plant workers filing a report with the police. We see Fabrizio Menghini rushing around Rome madly searching for Zio Giuseppe; and the four workers are ushered quickly into a meeting with magistrates. At this point, we must also indicate to our viewers that an ancillary investigation of Zio Giuseppe has already been assigned to the carabinieri. Up to this point there has been no direct evidence to link Zio Giuseppe to Wilma's death. Only suspicions. The scope of the investigation is to paint a broad picture of Zio Giuseppe's moral and financial character. The investigation is called "Operation Giuseppe." We should indicate this investigation is going on by a close-up on a series of files marked "Operation Giuseppe," followed by quick cuts to carabinieri tailing Zio Giuseppe through Rome. We may choose to film the "Operation

Giuseppe" antics in sped-up motion as an homage to Keystone Cop films.

Some doubts. We should recall that the carabinieri commence their investigation of Zio Giuseppe just around the time Silvano Muto publishes an article implicating "Signor X" and "Signor Y" in his fledgling *Actuality*. Zio Giuseppe, who apparently had only the most minimal contact with his brother's family, was often questioned by the tabloids about Wilma, in exchange for increasingly significant sums. Later, some witnesses will note that his loquacity around reporters may have been a serious miscalculation on his part.

Immediate family members continue to swear that Wilma never went out alone, except in the months just prior to her death, to purchase thread or other sundries in the neighborhood for her trousseau. They appear so vehement and rigid that people begin to wonder about them. We come to learn that for the past several years, the Montesis have employed maids. They also have a private telephone, luxuries for a family in their economic position (but, to be fair, they don't have heat in their apartment). As a foreign correspondent for the left-wing *El Espectador* of Bogotá, Gabriel García Márquez reports with poetic elegance on the case and finds that Signora Montesi is not well liked in the neighborhood around Via Tagliamento. She puts on airs. She uses profanities and behaves like the despot of the family. Shot of a reporter, resembling Márquez, tipping his hat to Maria Petti and Wanda as they return home from the market, possibly engaged in an argument. Shot of police listening to conversations on a primitive tape recorder. It is around this time that police place a bug on the Montesis' phone.

In *actuality*, the watchword of information technology in daily life, the bugs never reveal much beyond the ordinary speech of grief. Many journalists call with offers to help the family in exchange for information.

Voice of journalist: "The public in Rome is taking over the Montesi case, and is asking: 'Why couldn't Wilma's death be simply due to a *disgrazia?*' Sometimes what we are looking for is actually right under our eyes, like the famous purloined letter of Poe. Public opinion in Rome holds that the poor girl was abducted and killed. No one believes she really drowned while taking a footbath."

A detective asks Maria Petti for the names of Wilma's friends. Maria Petti replies: "If you want to know about my poor little daughter, who can tell you more than her mother? She had no secrets from me . . . I am my daughters' friend. Their only friend. My daughters confide in me. I am the only one. The only friend of my daughter. She has no secrets from me."

Wanda is also questioned about the issue of Wilma's friends and responds: "She had friends in a manner of speaking, but we two were the real friends."

If girls are kept indoors or are allowed to circulate only with their mothers and sisters, how will they meet young men? Perhaps only within the family circle itself. Or in highly controlled situations of surveillance.

◠

Flashback. A friend of Wilma's mother suggests she is too severe with her girls, so Maria Petti agrees to accompany Wilma and Wanda to a dance hall in Rome. Wilma is not particularly comfortable there. Angelo Giuliani approaches the Montesi party and asks to dance with Wilma. Maria Petti vaguely nods yes, and the couple waltzes together, under her watchful eyes. Wilma declines to remove her gloves.

Giuliani, for his part, offers a seamless narrative. He had been only once before to the Sala Pichetti. After dancing with Wilma (he testifies that she danced poorly, and could hardly move her feet), he accompanied the Montesi women home and asked for a second date with Wilma. In front of her mother and sister Wilma inquired as to his intentions; Giuliani responded that he wished to speak to her seriously and to ask for her hand in marriage. Ten days later the couple was officially engaged. There was no moment of ambiguity, no period of flirtation, no unrepresented moment beyond the light of the cameras, or better, no privacy.

Even privacy, which posits itself as the folded antispace of everyday life, the antitime to the timetables of parking meters, tram stops, trains, and work, is actually revealed to be constitutive of everyday life. Henri Lefebvre writes of a dialectical way of thinking about privacy, imbricated as fantasy in the quotidian, as opposed to a static, functional model of urban time and space. In place of the great collectives that have been made abject in the new Europe is the idealized home-dwelling, consuming couple. But we should add a new dimension to this dialectical model, the dimension of cinematic time and space, where even the most banal of private moments are potentially the subject of a constant filming.

Today, in the glare of the paparazzo flash, indignant celebrities demand privacy, and testify before governmental bodies that they simply want to raise their children like good parents with wholesome values. But in the Italy of the Montesi case, we see that this demand is already revealed as wholly inauthentic. We could film middlebrow *Evening Courier* journalist Indro Montanelli seated in a comfortable armchair and waxing moralistic about the imbrications of cinema and real life:

"There is much to say about this problem, and about the strange, new, phenomenon whereby all of humanity seems preoccupied with behaving as if they are in front of a movie camera. Intimate relations, such as between married people, secret feelings, jealousy, love, affection, laughter between friends, domestic happiness and unhappiness: everything today is material for publicity, material for a news conference, and material for the cinema. What is to become of that which the English call *privacy*, and which we, unfortunately, can only translate with a forced and arbitrary term—*privatezza*—since there is no exact equivalent in our language, and as the very concept is foreign to our manners?"

Montanelli goes on to link the loss of individual privacy not to the inevitable cycle of demand-production in capitalist (or film) culture, but to the infection of the West with socialist values, overdetermined in the figure of the camera. The protagonists of tabloid journalism belong to a *kolchoz* (construed first as a social formation in which the patriarchy loses its grip and paternal power is transferred to the trade unions), and more specifically to a "*kolchoz* morality" (translated in narrative terms to the figure of parentless children; or to the little boy whose assiduous industry contrasts with the attitude of his impotent father—as in *The Bicycle Thief* and many postwar films). Montanelli's rhetoric provides a frame in which to understand the anxiety of "intimacy" generated by the camera in neorealism. When we see the Montesi family agree to participate in a film project related to Wilma's death, Montanelli does not blame her father. Rather, in a fascinating turn, Montanelli blames the culture industry in general, a construct in which tabloid journalism, incipient forms of paparazzo-photography, trash literature, and the more "engaged" forms of cinema such as neorealism coexist without contradiction. Finally, the *kolchoz* is simply public opinion: "The *kolchoz* demands a film, a film that will lend cheer to the communal evenings." Montanelli understands Rodolfo Montesi as a father who acts out the "anticipation of this regime" unconsciously before the camera.

What did fiancé Angelo Giuliani know about Wilma? Was he concerned about her background? He responds to investigators: "Yes, I did ask around, to some neighbors of the Montesis whose name I don't remember. They answered that they were a solid family, of good reputation. They said the girl and her sister were good girls: in the neighborhood they were called the Siamese twins because they always went around together."

Once they are engaged, Wilma and Giuliani go out alone twice, once to the cinema, and once for a walk around the Villa Borghese. Well, what transpires between

Wilma and Giuliani? Perhaps, as Wilma once burst out, he "attempted to lack respect for her." Could this event have triggered in Wilma a panic, causing the delayed reaction of a suicide, months later? And why is Giuliani transferred away from Rome to the provincial barracks in Potenza soon after his engagement? Various individuals questioned during the investigations will refer to this transfer as punishment. Apparently Giuliani fought with an officer who made an unsavory comment about Wilma. Giuliani is described as a mediocre soldier with little chance for advancement. Saverio Polito, Rome chief of police, under whom Giuliani had been a private, describes the young man as indolent, always asking for leave, perhaps even more so after he met Wilma. Giuliani characterizes his relationship with Wilma as platonic, and from his testimony, their engagement sounds very dull to listeners, entirely "flameless."

Dino Risi's episode for the 1953 movie *Love in the City* parallels the first encounter between Wilma Montesi and her fiancé Giuliani. The voice-over narration explains that the camera has entered a Roman dance hall ("just like the juke joints and canteens of America") and has managed to capture life there "as it is truly lived." A young woman sits in a folding chair, literally overshadowed by the domineering presence of her mother. An assured, swaggering fellow approaches the pair and rather disinterestedly asks, "Dance?" The mother sizes him up and shakes her head no. Next a man of suitable appearance comes along, a man who defers to the matriarch, making eye contact with her, almost shutting out the daughter. The mother offers a half-smile of approval and the pair takes to the floor. The ritual bears a sense of inevitability. Of course the mother will veto the first man and accept the second, following the 1-2-3 rhythm of the dance.

December 1953. Establishing shot of the eucalyptus trees lining the median of the Via Chiana, draped in Christmas lights.

Seven months after Wilma's body is discovered at Tor Vaianica, and a second police investigation has been completed, the Montesi case is finally "archived." In theory, this means that the police can now hold a press conference and reveal the precise evidence that led them (twice) to the conclusion that Wilma's death was an accident. If anyone is interested. In theory, the family can achieve what we now like to call "closure," assuming such a concept is not too foreign to fatalistic Latins.

But there is one detail to consider: A mysterious young woman wearing a camel-hair coat has come forward to say that she can back up accusations made by Silvano Muto's article on the case. We will not yet film her face, only her back as she is es-

Maria Petti agrees to accompany Wilma and Wanda to a dance hall in Rome. Wilma is not particularly comfortable there, according to a family friend. Angelo Giuliani approaches the Montesi party and asks to dance with Wilma. Scene from Dino Risi's episode of *Love in the City*, titled "Invitation to Dance."

corted to the Palace of Justice by Jesuit priests and important-looking men in tan overcoats.

Yet Muto had recanted his article in his own tabloid, *Actuality*, several months earlier. With the arrival on the scene of this witness, Muto is brought up on charges of "tendentious reporting," because, in essence, his article called into question the integrity and competence of the police. His implication of Signor X and Y in a criminal act contradicts not one, but two police reports. "Tendentious reporting" is a punishable act according to an old Fascist law designed to squelch Communists, which is still on the books. Muto, a rather clever young man, hires two lawyers to defend him on these "blue law" charges of tendentious reporting: One—Bucciante—on the far right of the political spectrum; the other, Sotgiu, the well-known Red who defended the two left-wing journalists accused of libel the previous summer. The camera will pan across the two lawyers flanking Muto as the troika makes its way across the Umberto I bridge toward the Palace of Justice. The Castel San Angelo and the dome of Saint Peter's are visible in the margin of the shot. The camera may linger for an exceptionally long time on Sotgiu, reminding the viewer of his features.

Once before the magistrates, Silvano Muto is forced to reveal the real names behind the figures of Signor X—Ugo Montagna, an extremely well-connected business man, a Sicilian who bears the title of marquis of San Bartolomeo, and Signor Y—Piero Piccioni, in art, "Piero Morgan" a band leader, film composer and radio personality who plays "cool" "modern" jazz and, more importantly, is the son of powerful Christian Democrat minister Attilio Piccioni, whom we have already filmed when he was handpicked by President Einaudi to form a new government. Specifically, Ugo Montagna, who manages Capocotta among his other business activities, was for several years the lover of the woman in the camel-hair coat.

Her name is Anna Maria Moneta Caglio (she is known henceforth as Anna Maria, or Caglio, or "the daughter of the century" or "the black swan" or "Marianna the wild" or "the traveling saleswoman of truth"). It is now time for us to view Anna Maria in a slow-motion tracking shot, ending in a close-up, as she extricates herself from the grip of a photographer from the *Messenger* who has promised to protect her (ironically, exposing her to the lens of Tazio Secchiaroli). A journalist describes Caglio as exceptionally pale, with only a hint of mascara and no lipstick, "according to the latest Hollywood fad." Her performance is likened to Ingrid Bergman as Joan of Arc. She turns dramatically to face directly into the camera, and we become aware

Ugo Montagna, the marquis of San Bartolomeo (*far left*), leads a Capocotta hunting party.

that she possesses a sensuousness made for the movies, a beauty that is only just out of reach. Simultaneously, she appears as a symbol of innocence corrupted, a confirmation of our worst fears about the ruling class's victimization of ordinary citizens of the incipient democracy.

Secchiaroli's image of Anna Maria Caglio represents the actual moment when cinema and real life become indistinguishable. We could think, in this context, of Cindy Sherman's film stills, in which the photographer makes herself up in various outfits from unrealized films. Caglio appears to be reacting to something the press photographer whispers in her ear. Her reaction is both spontaneous and rehearsed, a contradiction that characterized the acting style of Anna Magnani (the star that could have saved Wilma Montesi's life—if only Wilma had gone to see her in *The Golden Coach* with Wanda and Maria Petti). Anna Maria Caglio opens herself to Secchiaroli, and so presents herself to our viewers as the potential star of this film. Like the public that expects more from her, we will come to be disappointed, and the tension between our desires for truth and Caglio's limitations will be played out during the coming scenes.

This is perhaps the first time that the viewer of the Montesi film realizes fully the intrinsic connection between the case and its representation as cinematic. The effect should be devastating.

Continuity shot back to autumn, when, as we recall, Silvano Muto signed a confession stating he invented the tale of drugs and orgies at Capocotta in order to gain publicity for his magazine. Now he finds himself in the odd position of having to back up his story, or risk losing everything. Normally such a trial would take months to set in motion, but Muto is arraigned within two weeks.

Under intense pressure, Muto does what no journalist in the post-Fascist democratic republic should ever do: he reveals his primary source, a young woman named Adriana Bisaccia originally from a small town near Naples. After she arrived at Termini Station from the provinces, Adriana found herself seduced into a world of drugs, parties, and cinema. Adriana worked as an artist's model. At first she was able to maintain distance from the artists, but when a young man tried to talk to her, she became ashamed of her nudity and fled the studio. She also tried acting and stenography to support herself.

In Alberto Moravia's *Boredom*, Cecilia falls naturally into taking off her clothes for the

Anna Maria Moneta Caglio snapped by Tazio Secchiaroli as she is "protected" by another photographer.

young painter Dino, just as she had for her former lover, another painter on Rome's bohemian Via Margutta. Dino narrates: "Now she was completely nude; or rather, she still wore what I would call the most intimate bridling: the garter over her thighs, the triangular patch of her panties on her stomach, the stockings on her legs. This bridling was, however, by now all messy and maladjusted, as if Cecilia, in stripping, had taken away its very functionality: the panties seemed to be rolled up, the garter had two of the four snaps undone, and it hung obliquely on one side; one of the stockings was held up by the garter while the other hung below her knee. . . . Truly, Cecilia appeared double, or rather, a woman and a girl at the same time." And after this, Cecilia becomes involved with an actor. She justifies her movements around Rome to her parents with the excuse of auditions for various rosy neorealist productions.

Muto's main source, Adriana Bisaccia, knew details about Wilma Montesi. Or did she? Perhaps she was at Capocotta the night of Wilma's death. Perhaps the two girls were on friendly terms, sharing lipstick and secrets in the bathroom. Naturally, Muto has no current address for Adriana, but he tells police she is a regular at certain so-called existentialist bars in the so-called magic triangle near the Spanish steps.

Shot of police searching for Adriana Bisaccia.

It is a fairly common strategy for the left wing to accuse the Christian Democrats, the party of the moral high ground, of involvement with drugs. During the early 1950s, Prince Dado Ruspoli, a Roman noble associated with the Vatican and the party leadership, was arrested at the border for possession. At the time, Italy was one of the only countries in the world to allow the manufacture of heroin, ironically, to the profit of certain companies that were started up under the Marshall Plan. (We should note that Ugo Montagna served on a commission to decide how best to distribute Marshall Plan funds.)

Montagna has a dog named Marijuana. A maid tells Anna Maria Caglio that Montagna and his friends sometimes ate dinner in the nude.

Scene in a store near Via Tagliamento. One woman says to another, "If they asked me about Wilma Montesi, my revelations would destroy half of Rome." A left-wing newspaper reports that there was a long-standing relationship between Wilma and this woman's daughter, a drug addict who was in rehab and had uttered Wilma's name in a stupor. It is later revealed that the daughter, Angela, is not under the influence of drugs, but is, rather, a patient at a mental hospital where she is being treated for shock after the death of her fiancé in a car accident around the time of Wilma's death.

Adriana Bisaccia finally turns up at the home of bohemian painter Diulio Francimei on Via Margutta. Soon after meeting him, she realized he was addicted to morphine. Now he's in detox in a Rome hospital. Adriana is taken into custody and questioned for an entire morning. During this time she smokes forty cigarettes. She denies any specific knowledge of the Montesi case beyond the idle speculation of the bars. Why, then, did she tell tabloid editor Silvano Muto she had answers? She responds, "In my films I have always played walk-ons. Bit parts, just as I did in the Montesi drama. But Silvano Muto promised me I would finally become one of the stars." Bisaccia had worked briefly for Muto as a copy editor, and casually told him her theories "just like everyone else." That is all. Bisaccia is released to return to the painter's flat. Francimei tells Adriana that in her sleep she once cried out, "Don't throw me into the ocean like Wilma." The painter swears that she was hooked on Stenamine around the time of an alleged suicide attempt. Other helpful Romans come forward to say Bisaccia is an occasional user of Simpamine.

Painter Francimei is finally released from the hospital and arranges to meet Adriana Bisaccia in a crowded piazza, not to renew their relationship, according to Francimei, but in order to determine who started a rumor linking the painter to the suspicious death of another existentialist in Milan. As he crosses the piazza to meet his lover, Francimei is arrested for drug possession and later incarcerated in a state asylum for the criminally insane without any traceable arrest warrant. Again, shortly after his release, he, along with other bohemians, are rounded up in an existentialist bar and issued a writ of obligatory deportation from the city of Rome until the year 1959. Francimei leaves for Milan. No one seems to care, and he is presumably finished with Adriana Bisaccia in any case. In Milan, Francimei organizes a highly successful one-man show, but he ends up fighting with another painter in an existentialist bar and is once more arrested for drug possession.

Audrey Hepburn's forays in the "empathicalist" bars and salons of Paris in Stanley Donen's 1957 *Funny Face* may serve as a ready-made cinematic model for many of the scenes in our film. *Funny Face* mocks existentialism with the bearded, lustful Professor *Flostra* (a hybrid of Sartre and flotsam?) and his evenings of international philosophy, poetry, and song. When Flostra, in black turtleneck (note: "Dolce vita" was a style of turtleneck) lunges for Jo (Hepburn, herself in black turtleneck and black leggings), he ceases to be a philosopher of "empathicalism" and becomes simply "a man." Of course, as "a man," Dick Avery, a photographer based on Richard Avedon (played by Fred Astaire), is to be preferred. This film exemplifies a certain way of viewing the world through a commonsense, cinematic lens.

In the meantime, tabloidist Silvano Muto's legal position becomes more and more com-

In Stanley Donen's *Funny Face* (1957), Professor Flostra entertains "empathicalists" in his bohemian apartment.

plex. Investigators learn that Muto's father had been a local candidate on the Christian Democrat ticket of Lazio (the region that includes Rome), but his name had been struck from the ballot because of opposition from someone within the party hierarchy. After some investigation, it turns out that the politician responsible for preventing Signor Muto's candidacy was none other than Piero Piccioni's father, Minister Attilio Piccioni! Although, as we know, Muto did not mention Piero Piccioni's name in his *Actuality* article, the public begins to wonder if the journalist did indeed fabricate the story about Wilma's murderer, "Signor Y," hoping that the name would become public as revenge for his own father's political failures. Some other voices will suggest that the Jesuits, who champion Anna Maria Caglio for exposing corruption in the ruling class, may have actually introduced her to Muto, himself a left-wing Catholic, like Amintore Fanfani, key political rival of Attilio Piccioni. We will never learn precisely how the first meeting between Muto and Caglio was arranged. Did external forces push them together? Did they conspire to bring down her ex-lover and his political quasi nemesis by filling in the X and Y blanks in his article? However it was arranged, Caglio's first meeting with Muto takes place in the office of a dentist, a friend of Muto's named Pescarmona ("harmonious fish"). Muto insists on this location because he feels certain Caglio is being followed.

Shot of Caglio sitting prettily, her ankles crossed, in a 1950s dentist's chair. Muto pulls up a stool to talk to her, and she flashes a big, toothy smile.

Flashback to January 7, 1953. Several months before Wilma's death. Anna Maria Caglio attempts to telephone her lover, Ugo Montagna, for two hours without success. We can indicate the slow passage of time by an extended series of fade-ins and -outs. Finally, exasperated, she hops into her Fiat 1400 and drives to his place near the center of Rome. (Montagna maintains a luxury apartment in the city and only sleeps at the Capocotta estate during hunting season.) Caglio parks outside and waits.

It is around 5:00 P.M. Dusk is already approaching when Montagna opens the front door for a woman. We can just barely hear him informing his butler, "we're going out."

Caglio immediately concludes that the two have been involved in an afternoon tryst, which would explain why Montagna had not picked up his phone. For an hour, acting like a photojournalist on a scoop, Caglio follows the couple as they drive around the city. POV shots in this sequence help the viewer identify with Caglio, a jilted lover out for revenge. She has ample time to study the mysterious woman's silhouette; the shape of her head, her coiffeur, her neck. The sun begins to dip below the horizon when, suddenly, Caglio loses control of the wheel and knocks down a pedestrian. Realizing that the man is not badly hurt, Caglio screeches away from the scene of the accident, but she has lost the trail. The pedestrian, meanwhile, has noted Caglio's license plate. Police track her down.

Later, Ugo Montagna promises Caglio he will "take care of everything." He apparently keeps Caglio a virtual prisoner in his apartment until he decides to dump her, about a month later. We will film her stumbling out of his building, holding only a small suitcase. A taxi pulls up and she gets in. We notice she is crying as she powders her nose in the backseat.

When journalist Silvano Muto first publishes full-body photographs of Wilma Montesi, Anna Maria Caglio believes she recognizes the dead girl as the passenger in Ugo Montagna's car. Can she confirm the identity of her "double" with mathematical certainty? The question is interesting, since it returns us, again, to the mutual dependency of Caglio and Muto as witnesses.

Let us review: (1) Without Caglio's story, Muto would have remained an anonymous, struggling editor. His article in his own *Actuality* magazine had already been dismissed by police as unfounded trash, and he himself had signed a confession to this effect. Moreover, the identities of Signor X and Signor Y would not have been made public. (2) Without Muto's story, Caglio would have remained an anonymous, struggling actress-writer-existentialist-translator–law student in search of a rich and powerful husband. She would never have approached her Jesuit confessor with a story of debauchery and corruption in the Roman ruling class, or if she had come forward, she would have been absolved of her sins, told she had a rather vivid imagination, and sent on her way.

Shot of Caglio and Muto, escorted by their respective lawyers and priests, waving to one another on steps of the Palace of Justice.

Final sequence of shots of the various protagonists in the case ringing in the new year: Wanda, Sergio, Maria Petti, and Rodolfo Montesi sitting in their living room making halfhearted attempts to be cheerful; Zio Giuseppe out with a raucous group of friends in a restaurant. Zio Giuseppe's fiancée, Mariella Spissu, is also there, with her sister Rossana. They are considerably more gay than the Montesis of Via Tagliamento; Silvano Muto with a group of young intellectuals in an elegant bar; Anna Maria Moneta Caglio and Adriana Bisaccia, ditto; Rosa Passarelli, drinking sherry with her friend from Ostia in Rosa's spacious, central apartment; Angelo Giuliani, Wilma's ex-fiancé, toasting with his fellow officers in a dismal barracks; working-class residents of Tor Vaianica in a seaside shack, huddled around a wood-burning stove.

CINEMATIC
MOMENTS

After the scandal erupts, an aspiring actress using the name Wilma Montesi "becomes involved with certain producers." In the language of the press, "involvement with producers" is equivalent to decaying morals. Medical examiners stage possible scenarios of Wilma's death in which young, aspiring actresses agree to play the part of the corpse as yet another means of exposure.

Several left-wing papers claim to offer evidence that the real Wilma was directly involved with "cinemaland." Reporters later admit that the actress in question is actually named *Bruna* Montesi, who may or may not have used the name "Wilma" in order to be noticed. Bruna tells reporters that if they suspect her of trying to capitalize on the scandal, they need only look in the Rome phone book, which contains at least forty different Montesis. "Yes, I am ambitious," Bruna admits. "But I would never use Wilma's name because that would link me with an aesthetic of bad taste."

A boy places flowers around a makeshift cross on the beach where Wilma's body washed up. Like the children in the "miracle scene" from *La dolce vita*, his gesture is simultaneously authentic and staged for the magazine photographers who capture him.

An aspiring actress plays the part of Wilma Montesi's corpse as photographers snap away, their pictures reminding us that no photographers were present "the first time," when Wilma actually drowned.

The Pope speaks. "Cinema must seek to meet its challenge in an ideal way while avoiding vulgarity or indecent sensationalism. Without doubt, the ideal film has the right to lead the tired and vanquished soul toward the threshold of the world of illusions, in order to grant viewers a brief break from their difficult realities; however, the ideal film must be careful not to invest such an illusion with reality to the degree that innocent viewers will be tricked into thinking it represents reality. The film

LA MONTESI NUMERO DUE

Roma. Bruna Montesi con Gregory Peck in una scena del film "Vacanze Romane". La omonimia con Wilma Montesi di questa ragazza che ha recitato in parti secondarie di alcuni film, aveva fatto nascere la voce che Wilma Montesi fosse stata in rapporto con gli ambienti cinematografici romani. In questi giorni Bruna Montesi ha rifiutato l'offerta fattale da un produttore di partecipare come protagonista ad un film sulla ragazza di Tor Vaianica.

Actress *Bruna* Montesi with Gregory Peck in Rome. She had a very small part in *Roman Holiday*.

A boy places flowers on a cross at the spot where Wilma was found.

A "double" plays the part of Wilma Montesi on the beach.

must also bring viewers back to reality, with the same sweetness that nature uses to bring us back from sleep."

Shot of a conservative journalist reading aloud a brief item for the Vatican newspaper. "Neo-Realism: An Item of Cronaca": "A director and two camera operators from a well-known studio were filming several scenes of low life around the areas of Termini Station and the Via Veneto. Suddenly the police arrived, and, unaware of the crypto-Marxist aesthetic, arrested the protagonist-beggar, only to learn that this beggar was a 'distinguished professional, a highly paid, insured, member of the actor's union, etc.' We should say: realism with a blemish [*realismo con neo*]."

Within a few weeks, Anna Maria Caglio is catapulted to a level of fame that would have been unthinkable just a few years earlier. Her renown is based on a paradox: she is absolutely available to the public, and yet she remains a mystery. She seems to satisfy a hunger for information, a void that preexists her. Cinema people want to buy the rights to a film of her life; others stake a claim for her infamous "memoirs," published in all the major tabloids. The memoir is a specifically female genre, a confessional essay accompanied by glamour shots of the authoress, and many of the women involved with the case will write them. Men who write memoirs are somewhat more suspect. Long memoirs are spread out over several weeks with a "to be continued" tagline printed in italics. Such memoirs are thus granted an artificial open-endedness; others are subject to recantations and countermemoirs: "Why I Lied in My First Memoir and Why I Am Now Telling the Truth," reads a headline from *The European* concerning a baccarat-playing witness in the case named Jo de Yong. The memoir always hints at ambition to cinema, and even though the authors are paid, the mercenary background is eclipsed, displaced by a rhetoric of honest self-expression. Thus the memoir appears to grant "regular people" access to an audience, so they can tell "their own stories, in their own words."

Above all, Anna Maria Caglio dreams of "cinema, and with cinema, celebrity and why not? A splendid wedding with a prince or a duke." A female reporter notes: "To avoid the spotlight [during the period of the Muto trial], Caglio will stay in a Florentine convent where, in the evenings, she will work on embroidering an interminable table cloth. Perhaps this tablecloth will form part of her trousseau; perhaps she will give it as a gift to her friend Piero Piccioni whom she met through her boyfriend Montagna. Although many mothers fear that their daughters will turn out like Caglio, in fact, she is receiving avalanches of proposals for everything because that is the prize one wins in scandal: Marriage proposals, offers for films, etc."

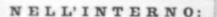

DICO LA VERITÀ DOPO AVER MENTITO

"Why I lied and why I am now telling the truth." Jet-setter Jo de Yong "confesses" on the pages of a tabloid magazine.

QUESTO PONTICELLO PORTA A CAPOCOTTA

r Vaianica. Jo de Yong sul ponte provviso-
o che porta dalla tenuta del conte di Cam-

fiancheggiata da mac-
e ginepro, nelle quali
Capocotta solevano an-
niali in folte comitive.

PERCHÉ
HO MENTITO

False le dichiarazioni all
stampa; non ho perduto 1
milioni al gioco; sono amic
di Montagna; ho visto il su
armadio segreto; so delle org

According to *Unity*, a technician on Valli's latest film was sitting in a café in Venice and happened to overhear her talking to Piero Piccioni on a pay phone sometime during the spring of 1953. Valli said either "So you did know her!" or maybe, "So, did you know her?" (obviously a key difference). And then, "you are going to have trouble for what you did to that girl!" To begin, we should note that there were problems all along in her relationship with Piccioni. On May 14, 1953, a little more than a month after Wilma's death, the *Messenger* published a tiny article at the bottom of the front page, bearing the headline: "Alida Valli denies rumors of her second marriage." (The question of "second marriages" was a hot one throughout the decade, plaguing Valli's friends Carlo Ponti and Sophia Loren, among other celebrities.) According to the article, Valli was not yet divorced from her first husband. "And so it is not true that she intends to marry a young artist from the radio, or even the son of a noted Roman political personality." It would not be worth mentioning this altogether unremarkable article but for the fact that the date of its publication, soon after the discovery of Wilma's body, is significant. In later testimony, Valli will never deny making the call to Piero in conjunction with her shock at seeing the tiny article, although she will say the film technician must have invented the lines he quoted for *Unity*. For now, let us remember that this phone call is potentially a key piece of evidence in the implication of Piccioni.

○

Anna Maria Caglio and Adriana Bisaccia meet for the first time at a press conference in early February 1954, and "the daughter of the century" invites the provincial after the meeting, Bisaccia announces that she, too, is preparing a memoir "in order to find a release for the emotions she has felt during this period." She clarifies, however, that hers will not be a "countermemoir," nor is it destined for publication (as if it were possible to announce publicly that one is writing a private diary!). She also warns that a weekly magazine is about to publish certain photographs of her in rather "indiscreet" outfits, but notes that these snapshots were part of a screen test and should not be taken out of context (as if it were possible to separate "real" snapshots taken "in context" from "false" snapshots taken "out of context"!).

Aside from casually recounting her theories on the case to Silvano Muto, did Adriana Bisaccia tell others that Wilma Montesi was killed by Piero Piccioni? Unfortunately, having suffered a nervous breakdown followed by amnesia, she cannot be more specific about the case. If there are any connections between Bisaccia and Anna Maria Caglio, "perhaps they are those links which unite all modern girls, those who never know where to turn with their anxieties." After the scandal breaks, Bisaccia dreams of returning home to her mama (who has not kicked her out, contrary to what "some left-wing papers" claim). "I no longer want to be a diva," Bisaccia explains. "As soon as the trial is over, my name will again appear in the papers, but this time in the classifieds, in search of honest work." As we know, amnesia is a common narrative device in soap operas, as it allows tired characters to start over with a clean slate; or it can serve to explain extended absences, lacunae, or what Catherine Clément called syncopes, forms (particularly female) of nonagency, self-eclipsing, cutting off from the Other. When the female returns from her syncope she asks, "Where am I?" But no one asks where she has been.

Flashback. After Adriana makes her "revelations" to Silvano Muto, the ambitious editor rounds up some of his trusted writers, and insists on driving the stenographer around Tor Vaianica, hoping to arouse some bad memories. Adriana grows increasingly agitated until she cries out, "This place makes me sick. You could die for being here." The writers from *Actuality* who have made the trip exchange knowing glances, and Muto promises Bisaccia that if she agrees to definitively link Piccioni to Wilma's death, the editor will set her up in Denmark with a new identity. He insists repeatedly that she must know the truth because she was Piccioni's lover. Well, was she? How does Muto know this? Did Adriana herself tell him? Does Adriana herself know the answer? Adriana feels she is losing her mind. She returns home from the trip to Tor Vaianica and searches out Piero Piccioni's number in the phone directory (we must recall that he is not yet famous enough to be unlisted, and his own father does not have a telephone). She dials. "Have we ever met?" she tearfully asks the musician.

He assures her they have not.

The developing friendship between Caglio and Bisaccia—a sophisticated northerner with aristocratic pedigree, and a southerner who is seduced into bohemian Rome linked by coincidence to the death of Wilma Montesi—could potentially have been the core of our screenplay. Unfortunately, the relationship loses momentum, the girls drift apart, and we are left without a sustainable plotline.

PART TWO
The Muto Trial

It is important that we avoid granting undue narrative prominence to courtroom drama itself, for that might give the impression that the judicial resolution to this case is a dramatic peak of the sort recommended by every handbook on the well-made screenplay. Since Silvano Muto's libel trial is brief, especially relative to the storm surrounding the scandal, we will only film scenes of preparation, marginalia, arrivals and departures, hushed conversations in the corridors of the "Ugly Palace," as the Ministry of Justice was often called. This overwrought building appears more complex than it should be, like the Italian judicial system itself, excessive in its attention to detail, but failing to amount to a fully coherent image. Photographers, microphones, and typewriters are banned from the courtroom. There are no sketch artists, so the public, like our viewers, does not get a visual sense of the trial testimony. Present are a prosecutor (representing the office of the attorney general of Italy); a chancellor who records (by hand!) the proceedings; a central judge who asks all the questions of witnesses (attorneys speak only through the magistrates, not directly to witnesses); and several jurists, all dressed in black robes adorned with gold braid, and white dickies. Eighteen Italian and two foreign journalists crowd around a small table. They also take notes by hand. We will show these individuals filing into the courtroom, and then the door will close abruptly on the camera.

The presiding magistrate occasionally announces press conferences in the corridors.

On the day that Ugo Montagna, Piero Piccioni, and Rome police chief Saverio Polito prepare to testify, paratroopers in full dress stop traffic around the Palace of Justice. A nearby bridge over the Tiber River is blocked off, and the piazza is filled with jeeps, armed tanks, mounted police, and trucks armed with water hoses. Five thousand reserve troops are on call.

Scene in which Piero's father, Attilio Piccioni, submits his resignation from parliament to Prime Minister Scelba. Scelba refuses resolutely to accept it. Shot of the two men wearing grave expressions. In fact, the Muto trial has spurred a series of political moves that are too complex to be fully explored in our screenplay. There have been calls for the Left to exploit scandals against the Right. There have been commissions established in Parliament to address the necessity of "moralizing daily life." Careers have faltered. We could indicate the severity of the impact of Wilma's death to politics by filming a scene of theatrical debates in Parliament with finger-pointing. In a rather surrealist parentheses we could indicate a right-wing deputy pointing at a left-wing deputy, who suddenly grows a beard and sports an Astrakhan hat. Returned to his original state, the leftist now points at the rightist, who sports the uniform of a Fascist Blackshirt. We could then move outside, where at a café

Reporters on motor scooters outside the Palace of Justice (the "Ugly Palace") during the Muto trial.

near the Quirinale, an English tourist reads the *Daily Herald* of London with its headline: "The Episode of the Drugged Girl Makes a Government Vacillate." The Englishman shakes his head in a mixture of disgust and amusement.

Scene in which a police investigator in the corridor of the Palace of Justice awkwardly reads from the black notebook in which Wilma copied, word for word, each letter she wrote to her fiancé, Giuliani. As the policeman reads silently, we hear Wilma's ghostly voice read aloud: *Here is one of my last letters, written on Palm Sunday, 1953:* "I am writing after Mass. How happy I would be if we could have gone together. Yesterday, after supper we went to the movies. I saw a film in Technicolor: *At Mid-Century* [a musical revue]. Very entertaining, but it would have been more fun if you had been there. I don't want to write anything that will make you sad. I am always thinking of you. A kiss. Wilma."

My very last letter is dated April 8, the day before my disappearance: "We had a nice Easter, except for the fact that you weren't here. We received your telegram at 1:30 P.M. You can't imagine how much it meant to everyone. While we were eating we talked only of you, and it almost seemed as if you were with us. In the afternoon my father's sister came with her little boy, and mama hid a chocolate egg for him. Around 7:00 P.M. Uncle Peppino came with his girl. After supper papa drove us to the Togni circus, near Ostia: we stayed three hours and it was very amusing. On the way back we took the beltway which brings us almost to our door. I thank you again for the telegram which we really enjoyed. I am keeping the palm frond with your letter. Everything that you give me is meaningful. Mama, Papa, Sergio, and Wanda send you their love. Your Wilma."

A medical examiner named Rinaldo Pellegrini, hired by Silvano Muto's lawyers, reviews the autopsy. Pellegrini notes that the vocation of medical examiner requires "mental orderliness" and "culture, and yet sometimes the Mediterranean genius prefers to exercise empiricism, if for no other reason than because it is less tiring." In other words, the initial autopsy appears to Pellegrini to be simply inadequate. Certainly, Wilma did drown. She was found with her jacket filled with sand, and there was a substantial amount of salt water in her stomach and intestines. (Interestingly, in Italian, the term for a cover-up is a "sanding over" [*insabbiamento*]). But she may have also been suffocated, and no evidence proves conclusively that she drowned at Ostia rather than at Tor Vaianica or that drowning was the sole cause of death.

Pellegrini considers "fantastical" the notion that the body would travel twenty kilometers in the sea. Moreover, he does not accept the footbath hypothesis. Why would

PART THREE
The Pause

The judicial inquiry is assigned to a magistrate named Raffaele Sepe, famous for having successfully prosecuted a maxitrial of money launderers. We watch as countless boxes of paper are transferred to Sepe's office, under five separate classifications: two related to the first investigation of Wilma's death; and three related to the ten days of testimony during the Muto trial. The documents are kept under armed guard, day and night. This is the same office in which, thirty years earlier, in 1924, magistrates carried out the inquiry on the death of Socialist deputy Giacomo Matteotti. Historians are almost universally agreed that Matteotti was shot under direct orders from Mussolini, who managed to remain unsullied by the affair. The Matteotti case is often considered the turning point in the institution of the Fascist dictatorship in Italy. There would be no turning back.

One of Sepe's first actions is to order that the body of Wilma Montesi be exhumed. A second, "super," exam is performed by "super" experts. The superexaminers state clearly that from the start, their work, however thorough, will ultimately only hope to clarify the cause, but not the exact time of death, given the extended period during which the body has been in the ground.

The superexaminers notice one thing that had gone unremarked in the first autopsy: Wilma's heart, or at least her aorta, is small, allowing for the possibility that, if Wilma did ingest cocaine, she might have suffered a collapse more readily than an individual with a normal-sized heart. On the other hand, the doctors also admit that the heart could have shrunk in the normal course of decay during the year following Wilma's death.

Many outside observers feel this exhumation is futile, since the only organs in which minute traces of drugs can be discovered—the brain and spinal cord—normally disintegrate within a year after burial. The superexaminers appear in absolute accordance with the initial autopsy on only two points: (1) that Wilma died by drowning; and (2) that a *disgrazia*, suicide, or homicide are all plausible hypotheses.

Sepe holds many private conferences with the protagonists of the Muto trial, including Anna Maria Caglio and Adriana Bisaccia. In a conversation with the latter, Sepe learns that the son of another Christian Democrat minister, Umberto Tupini, may be involved with cocaine trafficking. "Tupini's son asked me to distribute packets of cocaine," Adriana explains. "When I refused he threatened me. I was going to kill myself. I was going to jump off a bridge into the Tiber River."

In his episode for *Love in the City*, "Suicide Attempt," Michelangelo Antonioni draws very precisely from news stories of the period—not particular stories, perhaps, but in its

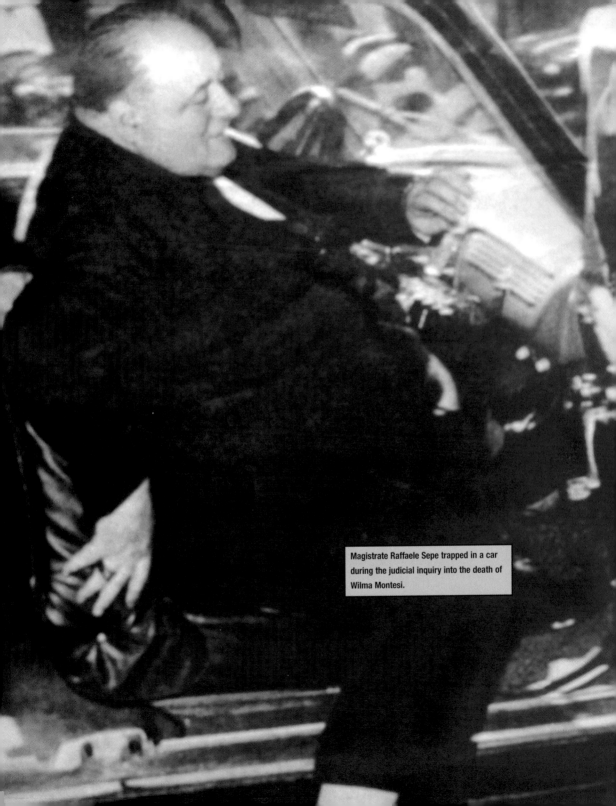

Magistrate Raffaele Sepe trapped in a car during the judicial inquiry into the death of Wilma Montesi.

very imprecision and generality, the episode evokes a whole aesthetic, a whole cultural production of feigned, aborted, and unsuccessful suicides. A young woman explains that she first imagined her death walking along the Tiber, seeing all those bridges. As she reenacts her suicide attempt, groups of men look at her, established as the diegetic gaze. She explains that a boy was fishing and we cut to his (putative) gaze, from the bottom of the stairs. He was frightened by her strange demeanor and ran away, she says, but at this point the camera refuses to obey her narrative and remains fixed on her. As she walks into the frame, we realize suddenly the presence of an investigator. At first he keeps a respectful distance. Then he jump-cuts over to her, a cut that sutures the cumbersome relocation of the filming apparatus itself. At the same time, the investigator's voice asks: "You actually leaped?" She describes the indescribable moment of self-syncopation, and the camera moves (as if embarrassed by its own clumsy presence in this moment at which cinematic representation reveals its own inefficacy) to the water. The narrative is put back on track, repositioned by a documentary-style interview with an expert witness, like those called to testify about Wilma's body.

Scene outside of a fashionable Roman café. Police arrest Minister Tupini's son. "We're taking you in for a lineup," they explain.

Cut back to Adriana Bisaccia chewing her lip as she scans a group of well-dressed young men. Unfortunately (for her), she is unable to identify Tupini as the man who threatened her life. The term for lineup in Italian is "American-style confrontation."

Naturally, Magistrate Sepe wants to know as much as he can about Muto's Signor Y, Piero Piccioni. Piero's alibi for the day of Wilma's disappearance takes a while to gel, but once the Piccioni family realizes the true gravity of the situation, they claim they can prove beyond a shadow of a doubt that Piero could not possibly have killed her. For a few days before the ninth of April, Piero and his then girlfriend, starlet Alida Valli, had been on the Amalfi coast, as guests of film director Carlo Ponti and his then girlfriend, Sophia Loren. Piero and Valli had been seen at a party hosted by Roberto Rossellini and Ingrid Bergman, at which stars including Zsa Zsa Gabor were present. ("Given this illustrious company, why would Piero Piccioni attempt to seduce a poor Roman girl like Wilma Montesi?" some people ask themselves.) Sepe goes back to review the first police reports.

Antonioni's "Suicide Attempt" episode of *Love in the City.*

siveness. It seems that rather than reveal his frivolous Amalfi plans to his strict father, and perhaps in order to protect Alida Valli, who, as we know, had not yet divorced her husband, Piero had told a little white lie, saying he was going north to Milan, on business. Once his true whereabouts were revealed, Piero claimed he had been on the coast until April 10, but then he changed his story, explaining that in reality, on April 9, he became ill with the flu and rushed back to Rome at near record speed.

○

In the early 1950s Italy doesn't have speed limits. Article 36 of the penal code specifies merely that drivers must use discipline and moderation. According to Italians, posted limits in the United States have *not* been proven to reduce accidents. Shot of a traffic expert in Rome stating: "Moreover, such uniform limits are contrary to the very nature of the automobile and can obstruct the flow of traffic. . . . In Italy, speed limits would impede efforts to bring our roads up to the needs of today's drivers."

After investigating the Montesi case, a certain Inspector Morlacchi, a Roman with a dry sense of humor, is promoted to the city's director of traffic. In the 1950s Rome has the highest accident rate in the world, at least fifteen times higher than New York.

○

Upon arriving back in Rome, Piero Piccioni says he called his father's personal secretary, who then summoned the family doctor and, finally, a series of specialists. (For the flu?) Piero says he spent the evening of the ninth and the next few days in bed. He could not possibly have been at Capocotta with Ugo Montagna and he has the doctor's prescriptions to prove it.

Many observers feel that the barrage of doctors with their signed and dated receipts is a bit of overkill for a healthy young man under the weather. Moreover, as experts note, Piero's father, Attilio, was also ill around the same time. One of the prescriptions merely specifics that medicines were disbursed to "Piccioni," and another one appears to have a doctored date.

Alida Valli continues to back up Piero's story. On the other hand, Carlo Ponti and other habitués of the Amalfi coast are not eager to talk. Ponti is attempting to obtain an annulment from his first wife to marry Sophia Loren, and any implication

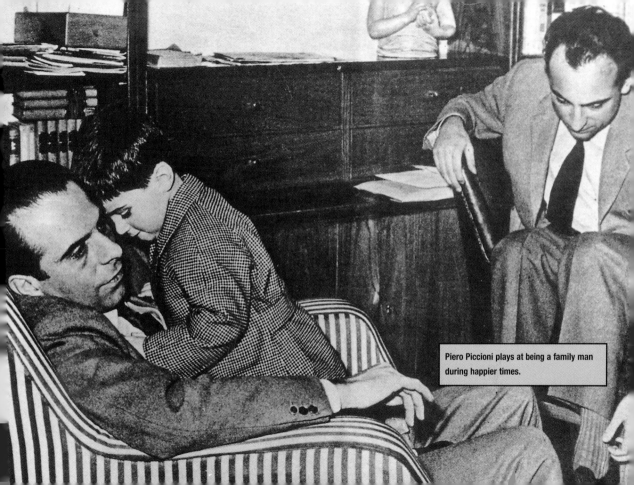

Piero Piccioni plays at being a family man during happier times.

As one journalist put it, Piero Piccioni made the mistake of overreacting to the gossip about his involvement, and his overdetermined documentation of his illness did little to clear his name. Even granting that Piero might have been a terrible hypochondriac, if the family did indeed keep such careful medical records, why didn't they recall Piero's flu when questioned as early as May 1953, only a few weeks after Wilma's disappearance?

○

Flashback to late April, 1953. Interior shot in the Piccioni's spacious Vatican apartment. A journalist learns that a right-wing humor magazine, *The Yellow Blackbird*, is planning to publish a cartoon of a carrier pigeon (*piccioni* means "pigeons" in Italian) carrying a woman's garter belt in its mouth under a caption reading: "Who knows what happened to Wilma Montesi's garter? Perhaps some carrier pigeon [*piccione viaggiatore*] carried it away." The journalist, who is a friend of the Piccioni family, resolves to inform the "pigeons" directly. She arrives at the apartment one afternoon in May, and she is greeted by Piero, his older brother, literary critic Leone Piccioni, and their two sisters. The journalist is immediately struck by their cavalier dismissal of the cartoon. She remarks that while Piero is a composer of "light" (or should we say "lite"?) music, for the sake of his father's success in the impending elections, he should not take this Montesi matter "litely."

This scene furnishes the opportunity to demonstrate some of the substantive contradictions in postwar Italian culture: after a while, Piero will remark that he should really make a phone call. The camera will pan across the living room, decorated with plush fabrics and mahogany bookshelves filled with gold-bound tomes. Abruptly, Piero will excuse himself and head to a nearby café to place the call. (As the viewer will recall, in spite of their apparent wealth, the Piccionis do not yet have their own telephone.)

Piero, in the café, speaks to his friend, chief of Italian police, Tommaso Pavone, in grave tones. On the other end of the line, Pavone assures the young musician, "You're not a suspect. Don't worry. Come in and see me anytime if there's more trouble."

Once again, let us note that at the time of the journalist's visit to inform the family of the imminent pigeon cartoon, Piero does not mention anything about his illness on or around April 9.

An associate of Tazio Secchiaroli, Sergio Spinelli, stakes out the home of Piero Piccioni, who heads out in a car and picks up Ugo Montagna. We should recall that at this time the two men are still claiming they do not know each other. Secchiaroli, along with another photographer, Velio Cioni, tails the pair to the Fascist Stadio dei Marmi, where they park, stroll down the broad avenue near the stadium, and engage in intimate conversation. Realizing the subjects are on a dead-end street, Secchiaroli simply loads his camera and waits for them to finish talking. As they return to the car, the paparazzo manages to shoot five pictures. The sequence reveals that the men grow increasingly irritated with being trapped by the photographer. Finally, they attempt to run him over, but he jumps out of the way, shooting the last picture at an angle. In the context of the narrative, these five images constitute a crucial scoop and help to establish paparazzo photography as an institution of contemporary celebrity.

So when and where did the name of Piero Piccioni first surface? Reporter Fabrizio Menghini believes that Piccioni's name begins circulating in Rome not less than two weeks after the discovery of the body, and only after allegations involving Minister Tupini's son (the alleged cocaine dealer and organizer of a dramatic anti-Communist exhibit) and the son of Rome's mayor, Rebecchini, have already been discarded. Even more significant in Menghini's version of events is the fact that Piccioni's name comes up *after the announcement of elections*, at a moment when the Christian Democrat Party needed to garner maximum support and when the right wing of that party was gaining power over the left wing led by Amintore Fanfani.

The driving force behind these first rumors may have been precisely the extraordinary speed with which the investigation was initially concluded. First came the supposition that there was "something more" to the girl's death, a structural space and a thirst for scandal, and *then* names began to circulate. We can indicate this confusion by showing men gossiping and smoking cigarettes in various corridors of power.

Did rumors of Piero Piccioni's involvement in Wilma's death first originate with the editor of *Tempo* magazine, Renato Angiolillo? He ran against Attilio Piccioni for a senate seat, and so could have held a personal grudge. We might take him as emblematic of a certain kind of opportunist in the early 1950s known as a *pastone* (a "big paste") as the Italians would say; a committed Christian Democrat of the Right at the time of Wilma's death. But like his friend, the director of the *Messenger*, Mario Missiroli, Angiolillo was not above changing his positions to suit the times. . . . Shortly after Wilma's death, Angiolillo has dinner with the infamous author and political figure Curzio Malaparte in Rome. Malaparte, who has been out of the

Tazio Secchiaroli's photos of Piccioni and Montagna

country, loudly asks his friend, "How is it possible that in a regime like this one, the son of a vice president of the Council of Ministers gets away with—"

"Where do you get off?" Angiolillo interrupts.

After this, the two men engage in an argument that grows so heated they create a spectacle in the restaurant. Later, when he is questioned about possible political motivations for starting rumors, Angiolillo cites this public fight, witnessed by many, as demonstrating that far from being the source of gossip, he was actually defending Piccioni; and besides, he adds, Gonella was vice president at the time of Wilma's death, not Piccioni. Curzio Malaparte, a man who at one time or another embraced republicanism, nationalism, Fascism, and later Communism, was dying of pleurisy in a Chinese clinic during the period of the Montesi inquiry. When a gravely ill Malaparte returns to Italy during the Venice trial in 1957, he is met at the airport by various friends including Angiolillo, Alberto Moravia, and Primo Levi. (Malaparte's fabulous house, willed to the Chinese government after his death, was the setting for Godard's 1962 film *Contempt.*)

May 1954, just over a year after Wilma's death. After receiving some two hundred proposals, the Montesi family agrees to the making of a film to be titled *Wilma Montesi.* At first, some members of the press report that *Wilma Montesi* will be polemical and will "put into evidence certain scandalistic excesses." The young director who manages to strike the deal, Sergio Schera, is not particularly well known. Like so many other directors who emerge after the war, he studied during the Fascist period at the Roman Centro Sperimentale, and has worked as an actor in radio and theater. His major directorial credit to this point is an animated film called *Ulysses and Polyphemus,* but somehow he impresses the Montesi family as being important and serious. As outlined by Schera, *Wilma Montesi* is to include a "documentary portion" filmed in the Montesi apartment, featuring actual members of the family (that is, starring Sergio, Wanda, and Rodolfo, but with a double playing Maria Petti, who is perhaps too modest to appear). Other scenes will be filmed at Tor Vaianica, but not as Ostia (suggesting that the screenwriters do not actually accept the footbath hypothesis that the Montesi family champions so vehemently in public).

Were the Montesis to receive compensation for their participation in *Wilma Montesi*? Inquiring minds want to know. (Shot of the Montesis walking through the Verano cemetery with Sergio Schera and pointing out the style and size of chapel they would like to have for their family.)

Shot of Augusto Carbone, a lawyer retained by the Montesis (for a possible civil case), angered that he has not been consulted about the film. He holds a panicked press conference at which he tells reporters: "It is impossible [that they would agree to such a thing], unless they went crazy over night! The behavior of Wilma's relatives has always been that of a family touched by an inconsolable pain for the loss of their daughter; they have been closed in their own world; in the last year they have lived a sort of mournful isolation; time after time they have refused to speak out; they have attempted to avoid the curiosity of journalists and photographers, when they were forced to go the Palace of Justice for interrogations; they have never given the slightest hint of wishing to capitalize on their misfortune."

Shot of journalist Fabrizio Menghini, still dressed in coat and hat, pleading with Maria Petti and Rodolfo to cancel plans for the film. Maria Petti collapses in tears. Rodolfo, pale, dressed in bathrobe and slippers, tries to comfort his wife and throws a pitiful glance toward Menghini.

The following day. Director Sergio Schera speaks to the press, explaining that, contrary to rumors, the family has agreed to participate in the film project in order to *counter* "certain scandalistic excesses." Schera reports that his film will bolster the footbath theory, although Wilma herself will never appear as a character. Other actors playing minor roles will be unknowns, or chosen from the world of theater rather than the "licentious" circles of Cinecittà.

The family confirms Schera's announcement, but attorney Carbone arrives at their apartment and declares the contract null and void, quickly beginning damage control with the press: "The idea that movie cameras, electric generators, carts, sunlamps, would one day invade the bedroom where poor Wilma slept for so many years, next to her sister, or the dining room where, the evening of April 9, 1953, the family waited in vain for Wilma's return, left us for many hours perplexed."

Within twenty-four hours, Carbone and journalist Menghini have arranged for the film contract to be shredded. Shot of bored secretary shredding contract by hand.

After the announcement and subsequent repudiation of the film project, public opinion seems to turn against the Montesis—especially the women, who appear compromised, as if they have been lured ever further into the culture of tabloids, parties, and cinema gossip sheets condemned by commonsense, middle-class, Christian Democrats. Shot of Wanda and Maria Petti as they are ushered into the Ugly Palace by guards to be questioned by the magistrate, Raffaele Sepe.

During the spring of 1954, the tabloids offer twenty million lire to anyone who comes forward with a photo of Wilma Montesi and Piero Piccioni together. This is the period

when photo-montage techniques developed by the avant-garde are applied on spec, and enterprising individuals doctor photographs for considerable sums to sell to the tabloids. No one, however, manages to find a photo of Piccioni with the carpenter's daughter.

Five photos of Anna Maria Caglio and Ugo Montagna dancing, from their "happy period," fetch two hundred thousand. By way of context, the monthly income of a middle-class family of four in Rome during the early 1950s is seventy thousand.

Anna Maria Caglio dances with paparazzo Tazio Secchiaroli in an outdoor nightclub near Rome, her dreams of a prince deferred. In the picture, Caglio appears slightly taller than her partner, and they view each other with amused smirks. "During the hunt there is time for fun," Secchiaroli wrote on the back of a print. Compositionally, Caglio occupies the dead center of the image, but if there is any *punctum* (to borrow a term from Roland Barthes) to which the eye is drawn, it is Secchiaroli's flash that protrudes from his cumbersome camera bag slung over his shoulder. Because of the reflective material of the flash, it seems to actually provide the light, as if it is working constantly, even while the photographer is on a break. At this moment in time, both Caglio and Secchiaroli are simply playing their respective roles while the other couples on the dance floor engage in more authentic and unselfconscious interactions. What emerges from this is the idea that the paparazzo shot is not a total image, but a sign (or a series of signs), a conspiracy between photographer and subject that is irreducible to the picture frame. The "celebrity core" of a paparazzo shot could potentially share space in the frame with alternative shots, just as Caglio and Secchiaroli share space with the more naturalized dancers.

Most of the cameras used by the photographers in the 1950s were rather large, with a separate flash unit housed to the side of the lens. Although single-lens-reflex cameras were actually developed in the nineteenth century, they were heavy, prone to breaking, and used 35 mm film (small format). SLR cameras were not favored by professionals, who considered larger negatives to be preferable. Instead, twin lens cameras, utilizing large format roll film, allowed the paparazzi to snap at odd angles, to hold the camera low to the ground, or even to engage in tricks to make it appear they were shooting in another direction. In most cases, then, the lens is disjoined from the viewfinder, and aggressive paparazzi were known to place postage stamps over the lenses of their competitors, who might not realize their shots had been blocked until they went to develop their film! The disjoined nature of the paparazzo apparatus becomes particularly evident in this shot of Secchiaroli, suggesting that the style of photography he helped

Anna Maria Caglio dances with paparazzo Tazio Secchiaroli in a nightclub near Rome.

to coin is one of differential planes, inconsistencies, inherent contradictions (as opposed to the smooth look of his later movie set photos). The paparazzo does not use detective or spy cameras (hidden in ties, or disguised as pistols), although these were also marketed early in the history of commercial photography. Instead, he surrounds himself with cameras, and is sometimes buried in them so that they form modular prostheses to his body.

Tabloids publish a photograph of Ugo Montagna with Christian Democrat minister Scelba in Sicily at a time when Scelba claimed the two men were not acquainted (the fact that the pair was pictured in Sicily would have deep connotations; recall also that Scelba headed the Ministry of the Interior in April 1953, and was thus in direct charge of police investigations); and another of Montagna and Scelba together at the marriage of Christian Democrat minister Spataro's son. Spataro, by the way, was a key figure in the development of Italian television and, particularly, the controlling hold that the Christian Democrat Party exercised over this new medium. It is also during this period—the spring of 1954—that Montagna begins to lose public support. His life is repeatedly threatened. An anonymous caller tells him that if he delivers a million lire to the basilica of San Giovanni he will be spared. Arriving with an escort of fifty carabinieri, Montagna finds the church empty.

Rudolf Valentino and other witnesses. A number of witnesses come forward to offer information about Wilma's death. For practical reasons we may choose not to include all of the following scenes in our screenplay—perhaps only a representative sample. The following anecdotes will appear, on the surface, to lack credibility. What emerges, however, is that the "character role" witnesses embody ordinary speech precisely because they string together various signifiers from the tabloids, creating new slight narratives, a term coined by Siegfried Kracauer in his work on realist cinema. Most of the truly committed neorealist films of the immediate postwar period felt morally and politically compelled to limit themselves to slight narratives, anecdotes from daily life without full closure or false coherence. The witnesses below link neorealist form with rosy neorealist content (a sprinkling of drugs, orgies, cars); that is, their stories exist as perfect analogues to the cinematic modes of the mid-1950s.

A dancer who goes by the name of Rudy Valentino confesses to Magistrate Sepe that on April 9, 1953, he took Wilma out on a raft in the waters at Ostia. Forgetting she couldn't swim, she dove into the chilly water and drowned. Rudy searched for hours, but there was no sign of the body, and he never reported the incident to police since he had no idea of the girl's identity. After spending a day in prison for false

Anna Maria Caglio, crowned "Miss Camera Lens" by paparazzi.

testimony, Rudy is released. Disappointed with the lack of attention paid to his story of the raft, he tries to commit suicide in St. Peter's Basilica by slashing his wrists. Normally when blood is spilled in a church, the space has to be closed and reconsecrated, but in this case, the priests don't bother. Rudy is admitted to the hospital for his wrist wounds, but leaves with his head in a turbanlike bandage. (Shot of Alberto Sordi in *The White Sheik* with turbaned head.)

Thea Ganzaroli, an existentialist from the Via Margutta circles, accused of "rather masculine tendencies," gives an interview explaining she had been making love *with a man* (!) on the beach on April 9, 1953. She witnessed Wilma's murder but didn't come forward because her lover was married. Detectives search Ganzaroli's lodgings, where they find stacks of letters from actresses including starlet Lea Padovani. Ganzaroli had apparently approached Padovani while the actress was filming a scene from *Prohibited Women* in front of the Trevi Fountain. Ganzaroli, speaking in "a low, man's voice" and dressed in "a rigid, almost military tailleur" asked for an autograph and wanted to be photographed with the actress. Ganzaroli then began to write to the actress frequently, begging to be invited over, until Padovani, suspicious of the tone of the letters, threatened to go to the police. Padovani swears to police that she never sent Ganzaroli any letters, so if any were found bearing her signature, they must be false. In January 1956, Ganzaroli will be arrested for kidnapping a pregnant teenager, helping her get an abortion, and then persuading the girl to live with her.

A country priest, Don Omnis, from near Parma tells police that a mysterious woman calling herself "Gianna la rossa" ("Red Jenny") showed up at his parish on May 16, 1953. She asked to use the priest's typewriter, and, after a few minutes, she handed him a letter sealed in an envelope along with half an entrance pass to the offices of the Education Ministry, in Rome, and instructions to give the letter to whomever came forward in possession of the other half of the pass. Without reading the letter, Don Omnis stamped the envelope with the date (which is significant given that rumors implicating Piero Piccioni were already in circulation, but not Ugo Montagna).

Apparently unaware of the grave nature of the letter's contents, Don Omnis did not bother to note the woman's license plate number, and she hurried off without offering further information.

Months later, on March 29, 1954, Magistrate Sepe receives a letter signed "Red Jenny," attesting to "horrible acts" committed by Piccioni and Montagna, and of their relation to drug trafficking in the region of Parma where Don Omnis had his parish. In fact, the priest had once been stopped as he rode his motorbike by police acting on a tip, but they never found any drugs on him. Red Jenny's letter to Sepe also makes reference to her earlier letter and the half ticket deposited with a priest of Parma the previous May. Now the magistrate contacts the priest and obtains the letter deposited with him. In essence, it says: "When you read this I will already be dead by the hands of Piccioni and Montagna." Red Jenny goes on to claim to have absolute proof of their involvement in Wilma Montesi's death.

Red Jenny never resurfaces.

A woman who owns a newspaper stall near the beach at Ostia agrees to an interview with Magistrate Sepe. The woman swears that Wilma approached her around 6:00 P.M. on April 9, coming from the direction of the beach, rather than the train station. Wilma asked for a postcard and a stamp. "I don't sell stamps," the woman explained. "But if you want to leave the card and payment, I'll have it sent later." At that point, Wilma filled out the postcard, paid, and moved back toward the boardwalk, away from the train station. By chance the vendor happened to glance at the card before mailing it, and she recalled that it was addressed to an officer of the police force in Potenza. This testimony is suspect inasmuch as the vendor did not come forward until after much material concerning the case had already been published in the press, including the fact that Wilma might have gone to Ostia to mail a postcard to her fiancé, Angelo Giuliani. In any case, Giuliani never received the alleged postcard. Shot of Sepe shaking his head and wringing his hands after the newspaper-stand woman testifies.

Investigators interview Jo de Yong, alias Giobben Giò, a rich South American woman who apparently told Anna Maria Caglio about drugs and orgies at Capocotta, and described sex with Caglio's ex-lover, Ugo Montagna, in vivid detail when the two women shared a table at the Kit Kat Club (featured in *La dolce vita*). Rumors circulate that Jo is a countess and a drug addict. Various weeklies search for her in Switzerland, France, and Spain. Finally it comes out that she is, in fact, an Italian woman, a gambler and jet-setter born Giovanna Giovine.

A witness who first identifies himself only as "Signor X" (not to be confused with the "Signor X"—actually Ugo Montagna—of Silvano Muto's article) writes a personal letter to Sepe stating that during the spring of 1953 he often took the train to Ostia in search of work. He and Wilma Montesi met after she dropped a stack of postcards and he helped her gather them together.

Shot of Sepe wiping sweat from his brow as "Signor X" mentions postcards.

It seems that Signor X and Wilma struck up a conversation, and Wilma told him that she too was a regular on the train to Ostia. "Signor X," later revealed to be Piero Pierotti, then told Wilma that he was planning to return to Luxembourg, where he had been doing menial labor and awaiting the disbursement of his veteran's benefits. Wilma promised to intervene with "highly placed individuals" on Pierotti's behalf. On their second meeting, Wilma proposed trafficking in certain "highly sought-after substances."

Pierotti was a parachutist and fought during the Liberation at the battle of Cassino. During the late 1940s he received a visa to emigrate to Holland, where, it seems, his passport had been burned in an accident. Serving as a witness in a judicial inquiry means that Pierotti will receive free passage back to his native country. When he boards an airplane for Rome, his temporary papers are stamped "self-identified" and the border police in Rome are waiting, so they can interview him upon arrival. Naturally, the loss of the passport not only makes Pierotti's *burning* desire to testify rather suspicious, but it also means that officials cannot verify his entrances and exits from the country to attest to possible drug-trafficking abroad under the auspices of Wilma Montesi. After giving testimony before Magistrate Sepe, Pierotti appears extremely eager to return to Luxembourg and asks for a diplomatic passport. He is forced, instead, to return to his home town of Perugia.

A man identified only by the initials F. T. finds himself in Rome, waiting in a parked car for an appointment. He is approached by a young woman who asks for his help and says she is being followed. She introduces herself as Wilma Montesi, and upon learning that F. T. hails from Verona, she sighs, "Lucky you. What I wouldn't do to get out of Rome! Here they are killing me, little by little." F. T. agrees to give the girl a ride, and as he prepares to drop her off near the Via Veneto, he becomes aware of a big black car on their tail. "That's my friend Giulio," the girl explains, growing increasingly agitated.

Several months later F. T. runs into the man he recognizes as "Giulio" near the seaside town of Nettuno (an area noted for drug trafficking—the obvious choice, in other words). Shot of Sepe playing with his handkerchief at the mention of Nettuno.

When F. T. asks about Wilma, "Giulio" responds, "Don't think about that girl. She is mixed up with very high people."

The blond playboy prince Maurizio d'Assia, nephew of Vittorio Emanuele III, last king of Italy, fears nothing. "I have an artist's temperament. I am exalted before certain Roman sunsets or before the spectacle that is Capri with its exquisite turquoises and greens. When I can, I chase away bad thoughts by taking a drive or playing some music."

After Wilma's death, Guido Celano, an actor, goes to Capocotta as part of a hunting party. He meets one of the guards, Di Felice, whose wife, Irma Mangiapelo ("Irma Fureater") had apparently gone to the beach to view the corpse on the morning of April 11. She had affirmed that, in her opinion, the death was no accident. After conversing with Di Felice, Celano receives a polite invitation from Ugo Montagna to leave the reserve. Some time later, Di Felice is interviewed by a reporter from a left-wing paper, and the guard explains that for a long time, he has had the impression that something untoward was going on at Capocotta. Specifically, he notes that he and his wife were scandalized because young people often went skinny dipping on the private-access beach (although assuredly not in early April, when Wilma died). Could these rumors of nude swimming have been exaggerated into stories of orgies?

The psychic of Rome declares: I have asked my pendulum many times, and I can state with certainty that Wilma Montesi was assassinated.

An ex–hotel clerk turned fortune-teller named Natalino Del Duca publishes a book on the Montesi case titled *Document Z*. His previous publications included *Proto-memoir for the Future: The Third World War, A Book of Science Fiction*, in which he attempted to arouse fear in the dominant class during a period when the MSI (Neo-Fascist Party) risked being disbanded under a special law in Parliament. Del Duca was a faithful member of this party and his book predicted that World War III would begin in 1953, with the Soviets landing on the southern Adriatic coast. It also states that Hitler was in the North Pole in 1950, disguised by a long beard because his assistants refused to shave him.

A disgruntled veteran, Del Duca notes in *Document Z* that he wore a Canadian woodcutter's shirt when he went to the Ugly Palace of Justice, in order to throw the press off the scent of his true identity. He is initially mistaken for a provincial or even a foreigner instead of the "true Roman" he is proud to be. Although he is careful at first, one day Del Duca lets down his guard and finds himself trapped by photojournalists who create a public frenzy. Citizens panic, yelling out, "Stop him! He's the secret witness!" or "Help! It's a Martian!"

Del Duca's revelations about a police cover-up, inserted at a particular time during the judicial inquiry, grant a temporary legitimacy to Anna Maria Caglio. But the fact that he is able to support her moral voice of condemnation seems to take a backseat to Del Duca's enthusiasm for implicating Italian police chief Pavone and other powerful figures. He raises the specter of possibility that Wilma's death was covered up due to an attempt to save the ruling party in the elections.

We could indicate the importance of the elections by showing Anna Maria Caglio in a flashback, lined up to vote, along with a large group of Italians, in the spring of 1953. In her vivacious way, she may begin speaking to a handsome stranger on line, telling him about her activities in Rome, about the origin of the "swindler's law"—the law to grant a parliamentary mandate to the party winning a simple majority—in the home of her lover, Ugo Montagna. As the stranger prepares to enter the voting chamber, we see a close-up of his hand. He wears a thick gold band on his ring finger. Caglio looks crushed.

Clairvoyant Del Duca is offered huge sums of money by various tabloids, and he finally agrees to sell an interview. After all, his involvement in the Montesi case had cost him his job. But even the tabloids end up disappointing him. After being promised money by *Today*, the magician is shunted to *Tempo*, a magazine that happens to share a lawyer—Augenti—with Piero Piccioni. *Tempo* publishes a much watered-down version of the Del Duca interview, which we should represent in our film as a fantastical vision, perhaps in overly saturated Technicolor, making him appear deluded about the potential force of his revelations. Naturally, Del Duca's response to this incident is to lament that he has no resources to hire great lawyers like the wealthy defendants in the Montesi case.

Unlike many of the witnesses who tell slight and fragmented narratives about Wilma, Del Duca forms his own broad theory about the case based on his ample knowledge of the penal code. As he notes in various direct addresses to the Montesi family, his version of events represents a logical compromise inasmuch as he allows that a criminal act had been committed, but he also preserves Wilma's purity and innocence. "How could the press allege that she attended drug and orgy parties, and yet she was a virgin?" Del Duca ponders. "Wilma, for superficial people, was both a whore and a virgin. What could be more monstrous, more absurd, than this connubial hybrid? Doesn't this violate the laws of nature?"

Del Duca has another solution. In *Document Z* the fortune-teller urges the Montesi family to form a civil party against Piccioni, Montagna, and Police Chief Saverio Polito, since, in his view, Wilma was the victim of an unsuccessful attempted rape. Yes, Wilma went out, like many girls. Yes, she was attracted by the glittery promise of the world of cinema. She made some contacts. She was invited to a party by the fascinating and talented figure of Piero Piccioni. Piccioni tried to have his way with the beautiful girl, but she resisted, so he drugged her. She died of cardiac arrest, struggling to save her honor. Her position is perfectly supported by the fact that she was missing her garter belt and yet remained intact. In fact, Del Duca reasons, Piccioni may well have attempted to put the garter back on, but by that time the body was too stiff. So instead, the garter was burned in the police furnace.

In this scenario, Piccioni appears as a healthy male, one who, as Del Duca reported, only took drugs occasionally and had several peccadilloes. Given this version, the only possible reason the family would avoid taking part in a civil suit is if they had been offered huge sums of money by powerful individuals. Of course, if the family does decide to bring a suit, this will bolster Del Duca's own position.

Finally, in his own defense Del Duca notes that far from wishing to ruin Attilio Piccioni, the fortune-teller considers the assassin's father the only decent member of the ruling party. Del Duca ends his book with a coda in the form of a letter to Wilma: "Your only mistake was being beautiful and believing in a dishonorable knight [Piccioni]. You were only a daughter of the people. . . . You were a genuine product of the Italian race, and above all . . . a Roman from Rome." (Like Del Duca himself, who is quite adamant about his urbanity and quite defensive about the fact that he was first seen testifying in the clothing of a provincial.)

Cheesy fade-out.

Cut back to black and white.

July 1954. Magistrate Raffaele Sepe turns over a sixteen-thousand-page report on the Montesi case to the office of the attorney general of Italy. It is unbearably hot in Rome, and the traditional month-long August holiday is about to begin. Shot of various protagonists from the case packing their valises with bathing suits and beach towels. Shot of Sepe's report on the case sitting on the desk of the attorney general. Shot of the attorney general packing a valise with bathing suits and beach towels. Interval of beach footage.

September 1954. Finally Italians have returned from their holidays. Shot of Raffaele Sepe reading aloud from his report on the inquiry into the Montesi case:

1. The rumors about Piero Piccioni's involvement began to circulate *before* upcoming elections were announced and must therefore be considered unrelated to a specific conspiracy to undermine his father.

2. Rumors about the involvement of Prince Maurizio d'Assia, and later, of Zio

Giuseppe, appear to have originated within Ugo Montagna's camp and are therefore not reliable.

3. The letters of Gianna la Rossa (Red Jenny) to the country priest, Don Omnis, clearly implicate the defendants. A suicide victim in Milan named Corinne Versolato had their unlisted numbers along with an article about Wilma's death, among her possessions.

4. Many witnesses saw Wilma near Capocotta on April 10, the day after her disappearance.

5. Anna Maria Caglio's revelations, while motivated by her desire for revenge on her scornful lover, nevertheless appear true for the most part.

6. Alida Valli telephoned Piccioni from Venice, probably on May 7, before she could have possibly received any clippings from the Rome papers gossiping about her impending marriage to Piccioni. Therefore, the phone call could not have been made to discuss the delicate question of the couple's engagement, as Valli claims; instead, she probably called Piccioni to discuss rumors linking him to the death of the girl.

7. Wilma's underpants and sweater would seem to have been substituted after her death. The panties appeared cheap in contrast to those normally worn by *Wanda* Montesi. The sweater was ripped and contained less salt than her jacket.

8. Various business associates of Ugo Montagna had heard that Piero Piccioni killed Wilma.

9. Anonymous letters, perhaps written by someone at the state television agency, implicated Piccioni.

10. Piccioni's amorous life was not as clean as he would have liked to paint it. He knocked up one of his father's maids several years prior to the Montesi scandal.

11. Piccioni's behavior after the crime was odd. He took no steps to clear his name, other than to sue a left-wing journalist for libel. He failed to comprehend the serious nature of the rumors circulating about him. He first told Magistrate Sepe that he had returned to Rome on April 10, and then changed his story. Could he possibly have recalled the dates after so much time had passed? Finally, suffering from influenza, Piccioni was apparently treated by up to six doctors on the weekend following April 9. He sent his father's assistant, the chief secretary of the foreign ministry, to fill a prescription. Several of the prescriptions presented as evidence may have been altered in pen.

12. The Montesi family had no idea of Wilma's whereabouts during the first days of

her disappearance. Rodolfo's telegram to Wilma's fiancé, Angelo Giuliani, read: "Wilma missing. Suicide suspected. Come immediately." The Montesi men combed the banks of the Tiber. Only after Rosa Passarelli informs them that she believes she shared a compartment on the train to Ostia with Wilma, does Wanda recall, first, that Wilma had talked about going to the beach to send a postcard to her fiancé, and, then, that Wilma had badly wished to bathe her feet in salt water. The delayed reaction and the overdetermination of the double-Ostia hypothesis offered by Wanda "were accepted willingly by the family of the dead girl, because this explanation fit with their desire to save the memory of their daughter from any suspicion."

Warrants are issued for the arrest of Piccioni and Montagna. The elegant marquis presents himself immediately at the gates of the Roman jail, Regina Coeli, but orders for his incarceration have not yet reached the prison bureaucracy. Guards attempt to turn him away until he produces an official document testifying to his arrest. (Meanwhile, shots of police detectives searching for him in the chic bars and restaurants of Rome.) In prison, Montagna receives meals from his personal valet. He exercises faithfully and wears a freshly pressed suit each day. Shot of a cheerful Montagna doing calisthenics in his cell in freshly ironed underwear.

Piero Piccioni stays in a paid cell. Shot of Piccioni composing at an upright piano as guards in the corridor smoke cigarettes and say, "The kid has something."

At a cabinet meeting, Attilio Piccioni formally bids good-bye to public life, stating tearfully that he must dedicate all of his energies to his son's defense. (He will return, once Piero's problems are over.) To put Attilio's resignation in context, Prime Minister Scelba also calls for a full parliamentary vote of confidence on the question of how he and his party handled the investigation into Wilma Montesi's death. Although the Far Left and Far Right form an unofficial alliance against Scelba and the Christian Democrats, the ruling party wins the vote by a narrow margin.

With the suspension of the judicial inquiry and the arrest of two powerful men, the Montesi family finally makes gestures toward a civil suit. In addition to their attorney, Carbone, they hire journalist Fabrizio Menghini of the *Messenger*, who, as we know, actually has a degree in jurisprudence. Menghini serves as a kind of moral advisor to the family, helping them deal with the press. He is also clearly in a privileged position to overhear conversations and gain the family's confidence, while he continues to report on the case on the paper's front page. At this time—the fall of 1954—no one has suggested that his dual status might represent a conflict of in-

The first photos of Piero Piccioni in prison, taken with a long lens.

terest. Shot of Menghini taking notes on a reporter's pad in the Montesi apartment. Shot of Carbone taking notes on a legal pad.

Having been given a taste of her vivacity, our viewers might wish that Anna Maria Caglio were the main focus of our film. We remain fascinated by her, but she is rarely seen. Indeed, she moves into a convent of Spanish nuns. Every morning she rises between 8 and 9; she takes a cold shower; does fifteen minutes of calisthenics in her room; and then goes downstairs to the chapel wearing the blue suit that she had on during much of the Muto trial. She drinks fruit juices and eats vegetables from the convent garden and buttered bread with anchovies. At her bedside she keeps a portable radio and two novels by Faulkner. When she walks through the convent gardens, armed guards keep watch at the gates. She receives hundreds of letters, and, when she does go out, she is besieged. If she is photographed she runs away, and so the press is filled with many images of the back of her camel-hair overcoat. Of course, even her presence in the convent is cinematic, but she has moved into a new filmic genre role: the pious martyr who has withdrawn from society.

After a brief stint in prison, Piero Piccioni is released on bail. He works hard on his music and keeps a low profile.

Ugo Montagna moves in with his father and attempts to reenter the business world, as he fights tax audits and a general loss of confidence.

Adriana Bisaccia abandons the world of Roman existentialists and sells cosmetics door-to-door in Sicily. Naturally, she would prefer to remain incognito, but occasionally a client recognizes her.

Every Sunday, without fail, the Montesis visit Wilma's grave. Rodolfo is hospitalized with an ulcer and the family has trouble making ends meet. Maria Petti breaks her arm in a fall, due to nervousness. Wanda Montesi is engaged to a worker from her father's atelier. A newspaper launches a campaign to help the Montesi family enjoy their Christmas holiday. The wife of the famous comic actor Totò brings gifts. Shot of Maria Petti fussing over her husband. The phone rings. Shot of police listening in as Maria Petti dares a journalist, "Go ahead. Write a piquant article."

Police suspect that Silvano Muto's defense lawyer, noted Communist Giuseppe Sotgiu, may be involved in scandalistic activities. Paparazzo Tazio Secchiaroli manages to catch the scoop, snapping a picture of the lawyer and his wife entering a brothel in a building that Sotgiu bought with his government pension. (Inside, the couple apparently enjoyed pimping young boys for Signora Sotgiu while her husband looked on.) Secchiaroli camps out, and after about five hours he shoots a

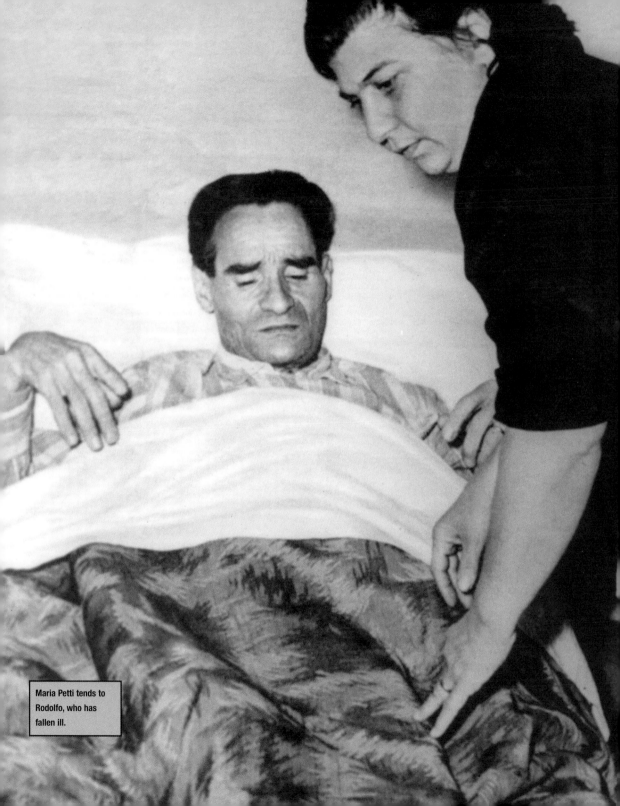

Maria Petti tends to Rodolfo, who has fallen ill.

second photo of the Sotgius leaving the building. But this time, the Sotgius notice the paparazzo! They ask him what he is doing. Thinking quickly, the photographer explains that he happened to be walking by at that moment and he recognized the lawyer. Sotgiu leaves, flattered and ignorant of what is about to break. Taken individually, the two images—a couple entering a building; a couple leaving a building—could appear rather mundane until we learn about their activities during the hours in between. What we need to keep in mind is that the paparazzo clicks his shutter under a certain pressure. He may not have time to think about composition or artistic value. The images become transcendental only when they are adorned with captions and laid out in a particular order in the magazine that has paid for them. The shock of the "before and after" photoessay lies, precisely, in the typography and layout; in the economic conditions that support the production of the pictures; and in the photographer's testimony of his own endurance.

☾

After a brief absence, Zio Giuseppe returns to work, and in 1955, he sues four of his colleagues at the Casciani printing plant for defamation of character after they assert to police that on April 9, 1953, he received a telephone call at around 5:00 P.M. and then asked to leave work, saying he had business in Ostia. We will hear more about this later.

Journalists offer millions of lire to the Montesi family for various articles and interviews, and they even help pay for Wanda Montesi's wedding. The family arranges for their sacristan to send bills directly to one reporter, who finally explodes to Maria Petti, "I'm not the one marrying your daughter!"

After a heated argument in the Montesi household, Wanda is subjected to a "prematrimonial visit" by a doctor. In fact, the very idea for the visit originated with journalist/lawyer Fabrizio Menghini, who believes that verification of Wanda's purity might calm things down in the family and silence gossip circulating in the press about the rather alarming speed with which the wedding has been arranged.

The doctor's visit takes place on the eve of the wedding. At 9:00 P.M. (!), Maria Petti, Wanda, the family's lawyer Carbone, Wanda's fiancé, journalist/lawyer Menghini, and another family friend file into the office of a female doctor. The Montesi women and Menghini go into the examining room while the others wait, perhaps reading tabloid magazines with the latest revelations about Wilma's death. Wanda kicks and screams with fright. A placard at the reception announces that a visit costs five thousand lire, but the doctor insists on more, given the late hour. Menghini pays, in cash. To calm Wanda the doctor says, "Miss, if you only knew how many other girls come here for the same reason!"

Afterward the doctor signs an official document that Menghini purchased in a nearby pharmacy, stating that Wanda is in a state of perfect integrity. The party returns home, and Carbone, the family's lawyer, places the document in a safe in case it should be necessary to make it public. Wanda continues to cry and goes to bed early.

Maria Petti feels remorse at having subjected her daughter to such a test, and Wanda has swollen eyes as she walks down the aisle the next morning. Menghini is a guest at the intimate ceremony.

Cut to Zio Giuseppe who has not been invited, reading a tabloid at home.

Once Wanda is married, Rodolfo moves to Wanda's old cot in the dining room while Maria Petti sleeps in Wilma's so that the newlyweds will have a double bed—the very bed that Rodolfo made with his own hands for *his* wedding night.

Wilma's ex-fiancé, Angelo Giuliani, marries the daughter of a watchmaker in the small town of Potenza where he is stationed.

Rome police chief Saverio Polito continues to maintain his innocence after his forced retirement under direct orders from the new minister of the Interior, left-wing Catholic Amintore Fanfani.

Suits and countersuits. It would be difficult to represent in purely cinematic terms the sheer bulk of legal activity associated with the Montesi case, charges of libel and defamation, the flexing of new muscles associated with the birth of the "free" press. We could indicate this significant social phenomenon by showing lawyers carrying dossiers under their arms, bumping into one another as they clog up the corridors of the Ugly Palace.

Caglio has dozens of suits against her during the decade of the 1950s, including one by her former lover, Montagna, one by Piccioni, one by Police Chief Polito, and one by a count named Francesco di Campello who owned a villa close to Capocotta that was tangentially linked with drugs in Muto's *Actuality* article. According to Caglio, once when she and Montagna passed the Countess Campello driving on the road that links the two villas, Montagna noted: "She is an idiot. I slept with her three years ago."

The Montesi family sues various left-wing papers, not because they defame the family name, but because they speak of a kind of *omertà* in the government. It is almost as if the family's patriotic sense has been offended. The Montesis sue writer Indro Montanelli and his famous editor Leo Longanesi over an odd book called *Addio, Wanda!* written during the period of the "pause," after Magistrate Sepe had submitted his findings and the office of the attorney general was weighing further actions in the case. The book is about an imaginary visit to Italy by Dr. Kinsey, at the invitation of American ambassador Clare Booth Luce (her term corresponded almost perfectly with the dates of the Montesi scandal) to diagnose the cause of the country's sexual lethargy, and to help Italy overcome its moral, economic, and political problems (e.g. to get Italy into NATO and into a strategically advantageous position for America) after the "near communist crisis" of 1955.

Shot of Indro Montanelli's "fictional" Kinsey concluding his report with the following words: "In Italy a swing of the ax against the brothels has destroyed the entire social edifice based on three fundamental points: Catholic Faith, the Fatherland, and the Family. Because it was in the whorehouses that these three great institutions found their most secure guarantee." Montanelli implies that without brothels, Italian families will cede to the power of "society," a mass of individuals without faith. "Moreover, in Italy, there is vice. There is Capocotta. There are girls dying on the beaches. Virgins, yes, but only in one sense." At the end of the book Kinsey directly addresses Ambassador Luce: "In the name of the Atlantic Pact, choose! The Italy of the pale faces or the Italy of ruddy complexions? The Italy of [the good whore] Wanda, or the Italy of Wilma Montesi?"

Caglio is finally signed to star in a film titled *The Girl of Via Veneto*. She plays a laundress from the working-class Trastevere neighborhood who dreams of a career in film or television. The laundress falls prey to the casting couch of a big producer with an expensive car, but finally, after various mishaps, she decides to return to her laundry and her simple butcher-boyfriend. (The displacements implied here are incredible, since she is only briefly "of" the Via Veneto, and then only for the most compromised portion of the narrative.) The film plays for one day in Rome and earns only eight million lire, half of Caglio's own salary. The film's producer declares bankruptcy. Caglio buys herself a blue Ford with her earnings, but she's forced to sell it after several traffic accidents.

Caglio later writes her autobiography, *A Daughter of the Century*, in which she blames her broken family for her problems. The book, printed at Caglio's own expense with her photograph on the cover, will sell only four thousand copies. Indro Montanelli writes an editorial for the *Evening Courier* stating that his parents were never unfaithful to each other and thus his mother could not have produced an illegitimate child fathered by "the century," nor would they ever dare to shunt the burdens of raising modern children to the tutelage of "the century."

PART FOUR
The Venice Trial

VENICE, JANUARY 21, 1957

The Montesi trial has been moved from Rome to Venice to maintain public order.

This trial spans several months. Like Rome, Venice is highly cinematic, but in a different sense. Venice is brooding and melancholic and lacks the wide-open spaces of Rome's sweeping, sunny piazzas. Instead, the camera must wind through labyrinthine streets and waterways, perhaps getting lost in blind alleys. Paparazzi surprise protagonists in our film by hiding under bridges and trap them emerging from boats. We will encounter heaps of garbage as we roam around the city. Venice is chilly in winter, and the piazzas are often flooded. Our screenplay will reflect the change in tone that comes with the change of venue.

The court is presided over by a president, a man named Tiberi. Scores of potential witnesses write to him, begging to testify. Girls claiming to be Red Jenny (the woman who deposited a mysterious envelope with country priest Don Omnis) surface, asking to meet with the president in his chambers. The rough Italian equivalent of a public prosecutor is the public minister. In this case, the P.M. is Cesare Palminteri, who is directly responsible for trying the case on behalf of the state. Neither Tiberi nor Palminteri were involved in the trial of Silvano Muto or earlier investigations related to the case. Palminteri's role becomes increasingly complicated during the Venice trial, and he ends up leading lines of interrogation that actually bolster the defense. Italian public ministers logically are "one and many": one in the sense that they represent the state; many that each minister is held to obey his own conscience and may, in fact, disagree with magistrates who come before or after him. We should keep in mind that Palminteri's role from the outset is to prosecute those named in Raffaele Sepe's judicial inquiry. But if, after hearing testimony, the public minister feels the original defendants are not guilty, he has the power to investigate *another* possible suspect. Italian law lacks what could be considered the single most cinematic element of Anglo-Saxon courts, not to mention a crucial legal element—cross examination. On the other hand, we might develop certain key scenes around the rather dramatic Italian practice of placing witnesses "in confrontation" with other witnesses, in order to allow for contradictions or retractions to emerge.

Of course, it will be impossible to represent the various juridical positions (even an Italian audience might have difficulty keeping them straight) in purely cinematic terms. Instead, we should proceed with the trial (we will intuit what is happening when fingers are pointed; we could even dispense with sync-sound and simply employ background music during some testimony), focusing our attention on the implications of the displacement of activity to the "politically neutral" city of Venice. Italy is a relatively small country, but unlike France, with its hub of Paris and radiating spokes reaching to the provinces, the crucial spatial-geographical code is that of North and South, Up and Down. Indeed, at the time of the trial, Northern Italy is still known as "High Italy" (*alta Italia*).

The parties who travel Up to Venice to participate in the trial all take trains. They do not enjoy the kind of individualized mobility of the fast car (Piero Piccioni speeding from the Amalfi coast to Rome with the flu). The train, not yet fully modernized in Italy, lurches along, carrying passengers through space according to a three-class system. It is interesting that we never see any trains in *La dolce vita*, although Moraldo, the character who is transformed into journalist Marcello Rubini, leaves his seaside town on a train bound for Rome in Fellini's *I vitelloni* (made in 1953, and released just after Wilma's death). In *La dolce vita*, the only person constrained by train schedules is Marcello's father, who decides to return home to the provinces early in the morning after he realizes he is out of place in the city.

A few nights before the trial begins, twelve teletype machines for reporters have to be delivered—no easy task. Workers wait until high tide—late at night—to unload the machines on the Calle della Sicurità near the Rialto.

The state charges the following individuals:

Piero Piccioni, for aggravated manslaughter in the death of Wilma Montesi (since Magistrate Sepe was not certain whether the charge should be murder or manslaughter, the principle of *favor rei* led to the lesser charge)

Ugo Montagna, for coconspiring, and for hindering the investigation into Wilma's death

Police Chief Saverio Polito for conspiracy and abuse of public office

Adriana Bisaccia for simulation of a crime that did not take place (this charge refers to her story about cocaine dealers, including the son of Christian Democrat minister Tupini, who threatened to kill her if she refused to make deliveries to customers); and for obstruction of justice in the Montesi case. (This charge is primarily based on Sepe's assumption that she is the author of an anonymous letter sent to a journalist. The letter explains that Adriana Bisaccia is a good girl who was "forced by hunger to make certain revelations and to write those memoirs" and who was madly in love with Piero Piccioni with whom she had a long relation. "I don't know if the story about the baby she had by him is true," the letter reveals, "but it is true that she still loves him and he still writes to her that he loves her." Sepe learned that the letter was typed on a typewriter belonging to a rooming house where Bisaccia lived, and the prose contains certain of Bisaccia's pet phrases, although she absolutely denied any knowledge of the matter.)

A series of other defendants face minor charges:

Pierino Pierotti, the unfortunate soul who lost his passport in a fire in Holland, charged with perjury. A spotlight searches for him in the courtroom, but a clerk announces that he recently died in a car accident.

Francesco Tannoia, who, like Pierino Pierotti, claimed to have met Wilma in compromised circumstances

Mercedes Borgatti, for inciting Thea Ganzaroli, the "existentialist of rather masculine tendencies," to give false testimony that she later recanted. Borgatti helped Ganzaroli write an article titled "I Saw Them Carrying the Body of Wilma Montesi" published in Silvano Muto's *Actuality*. Since Ganzaroli had retracted the contents of the article, she was acquitted before the trial, but Borgatti can still be prosecuted as the inflammatory article did, in fact, appear in print.

Michele Simola, an illiterate drug dealer who saw a picture of Wilma in prison and later dictated a memoir to his cell mates about Wilma's involvement in a ring of traffickers

Pasquale Venuti, who swore that a car in which Wilma was riding hit his motorcycle. In the fracas which supposedly ensued, Venuti saw a powder that he took for cocaine fall from Wilma's purse.

Maddalena Caramello, who testified that she repeatedly witnessed Wilma Montesi and Ugo Montagna together between April and June 1952 in a hotel in Rome. Again, we search for Caramello until we learn that she has passed away in the time since the charges were brought.

Four guards who lived on the grounds of Capocotta in the spring of 1953 are charged with perjury after their testimony during the judicial inquiry. In particular, they are held responsible for bringing suspicion against Prince d'Assia and creating general confusion. Many other witnesses who perjured themselves during the investigations or the Muto trial have the good sense to recant their testimony and avoid further prosecution.

The first session of the trial begins promptly, just after 9:00 A.M. on January 21, 1957. Journalists arrive early to be sure they find seats. But the court is "egregiously well-organized" as one reporter notes, contrasting it with the situation in Rome. On the first day, the public is lighter than expected, perhaps because Venetians realize that the magistrates will be primarily occupied with juridical formalities in the beginning. Along with the defendants we must cast twenty-four lawyers (including one woman), and at least a hundred and fifty journalists and photographers. The teletype machines remain on board a bus that is being used to block off the Calle below the courthouse. In theory, this trial should be the height of drama. In a traditional film, the lawyers would be dashing, perhaps a bit rumpled from lack of sleep, the music suspenseful, the outcome shocking. But our compulsion to remain faithful to the actual events forces us to compromise: we must represent the trial as rather tedious, dominated by the less glamorous actors who fight off colds in the persistent drizzle. Above all, we must make do, except for a brief appearance, without Anna Maria Caglio, who earlier seemed as if she'd been (self-)cast as the star of our film.

Shot of Anna Maria Caglio, doing pliés before a mirror in her convent cell.

○

As the gavel is lowered, the defense lawyers begin by asking that the court try the three "protagonists" separately from the minor defendants, whom Piccioni's lawyer terms "tropical vegetation." We should cast these roles with character actors; perhaps a cameo for an aging star who has been out of the limelight. The court breaks to deliberate on the issue of separating the defendants, and Piccioni chats informally with journalists, confirming that he plans to have his piano transported to the suite of rooms he's rented from a countess on the Grand Canal for the duration of the trail. "It isn't true," Piccioni announces, "that I intend to move to the United States after this is all behind me. If possible, I would like to go there every once in a while. That's all. I would love to play with Stan Kenton's orchestra, for example."

Wanda Montesi has a baby and is pregnant with a second child as the trial begins.

Wilma's younger brother, Sergio, has been forced to drop out of school, as his classmates continually teased him about the scandal.

The Montesis remain silent during the first day of testimony. Rodolfo and Maria Petti had last been to Venice thirty years earlier, on the occasion of their honeymoon. After much debate, the family has agreed to form a civil party in the trial, allegedly for the sole purpose of defending the memory of their daughter. Since the party does not present its case in opening arguments, the family's exact position remains ambiguous to many observers. Have they been paid to keep quiet? Have they finally

Five women stop in front of a makeshift shrine for Wilma Montesi in Venice.

renounced the footbath theory and do they now concur with the homicide presumption? If so, why have they changed their minds?

The court reconvenes and the magistrates announce their decision *not* to honor the request of defense lawyers to separate the major defendants from the minor ones. While charges are being read against Michele Simola and Pasquale Venuti, who claimed they were involved with Wilma in drug trafficking activities, a deep sigh is heard in the court and Maria Petti begins to weep. Later that night, the Montesis are spotted boarding a train back to Rome.

Scene in which journalist Fabrizio Menghini attempts to interview Maria Petti at her home. Wilma's mother typically suffers crises of nerves that make her petulantly silent, or she babbles nonsensically. Menghini pleads with Maria Petti: "The public believes you have signed a *pactum scelaris*; that you were told to keep quiet in exchange for money. If you want to clear your name—you know more than anyone what happened. . . ." Maria Petti simply stares blankly ahead.

Our screenplay cannot possibly reconstruct all of the Venice trial testimony. Instead, we should focus on key moments:

A certain Signora Gionni was employed for a time by the Montesis as a maid. She offers the most damaging testimony to Wilma's character of any witness. An extremely short woman, about twenty-five years old, Gionni appears wearing a torn red cape. She leaves her infant child in the coatroom, and she cuts such a pathetic figure that several of the journalists following the trial discreetly put together a collection for her. She confirms that she worked for the Montesis for about four months in 1952. Gionni seems not to comprehend many of the questions directed to her by the court president. She remarks that Wilma and Wanda always went out together, but then states emphatically that for a period of time prior to her death, Wilma went out alone every afternoon. She also apparently changed clothes between the morning and the afternoon; sometimes two or three times a day. Gionni swears that men periodically telephoned for Wilma or Wanda speaking in "grave" tones. (In *Boredom* Moravia explains how a young girl could receive telephone calls at home with relative discretion: "The phone was at the end of the hallway, at the darkest point, on a small table . . . as if she wanted to hide and defend the black ebony receiver from me, she turned her back suddenly . . . I noted that Cecilia responded with monosyllables or words even more insignificant than those she normally used, if that were possible.")

Gionni overheard various family members mention that Wilma was not in love with her fiancé. She overheard swearing and fights. Gionni claims that the Montesi girls

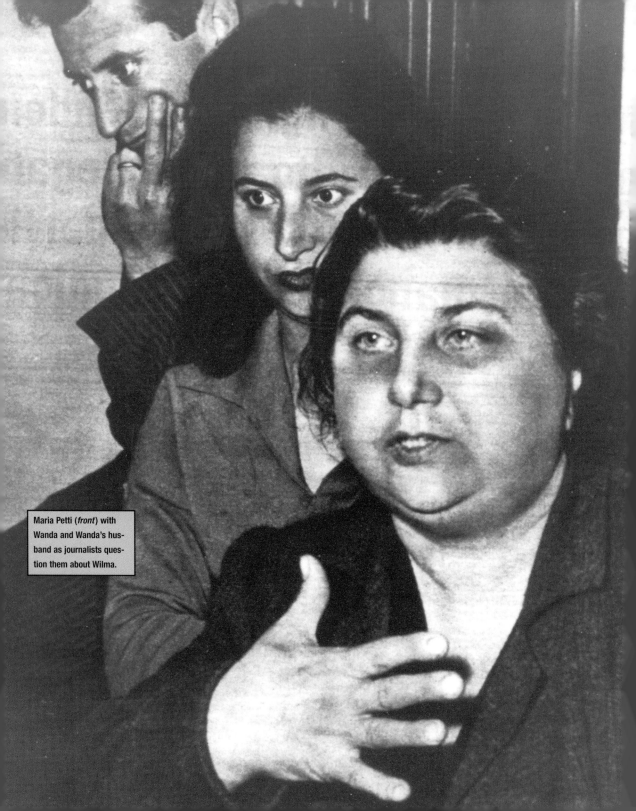

Maria Petti (*front*) with Wanda and Wanda's husband as journalists question them about Wilma.

had foreign perfumes (a fact that Wanda vehemently denies, quipping: "How could she recognize a foreign word on the label if she doesn't know how to read?").

Finally, under pressure from the court, Gionni has to admit that she left the Montesis house because she was pregnant (she was "interesting," to translate literally an Italian expression), something she did not want to appear in the tabloids, given that she was unmarried.

Alida Valli's testimony adds star quality to the Venice trial. Scene of Alida Valli testifying on the stand in Hitchcock's *Paradine Case*. In this film, she plays an Italian woman with a tarnished past, accused of murdering her rich British husband. In contrast with the real Alida Valli, Mrs. Paradine maintains perfect poise before the English magistrates.

During her appearance in Venice, Valli avoids contact with Piero Piccioni and expresses no nostalgia for their relationship. She feels a deep sense of bitterness at having been drawn into the case. She laments the fact that she didn't work after her name was involved, until, finally, Visconti decided to cast her in *Senso*, helping to revive her career.

Back in the spring of 1953 she *was* in Venice working on a film called *The Stranger's Hand* (based on a paragraph submitted by Graham Greene to a Graham Greene parody contest [he won second prize]) when she telephoned Piero Piccioni from a bar on the Giudecca. The question of the dates and purpose of the call remains tangled. She asserts that she may have called Piero to talk to him about various false notices that were appearing in newspapers like the *Messenger*, hinting at their impending marriage.

Valli no longer sees Piccioni or any other friends from "that period."

Scene in front of the central train station in Venice. Two police officers grab a sixteen-year-old runaway from Trieste. She explains that her parents wouldn't let her go out dancing, and so she left home, hoping to attend the trial of Wilma Montesi's assassins.

Italian pop star Ruccione writes a song called "Wilma." Street singers buy the music in a frenzy. The final refrain goes, "Wilma, only the sea and the night know the final word of your fatal destiny."

Police Chief Saverio Polito testifies wearing his two silver medals of commendation and the pin of wounded war veterans. He appears tired, nervous, and self-contradictory. He is asked at great length to clarify his relationship with fellow Sicilian Ugo Montagna. Polito maintains that the two men did shake hands, but that this gesture should not be taken as symbolic of a pact of *omertà*. They were simply introduced by mutual acquaintances.

Alida Valli (or simply "Valli," as she was credited) on the stand in Hitchcock's *Paradine Case.*

Montagna's testimony in Venice appears to observers solid and coherent, particularly in contrast with the aging Polito's. One journalist notes, however, a certain smugness, an immodest elegance in Montagna's manner of dressing, a self-pleased way of exaggerating his Sicilian cadence and a tendency to swear on his father's grave too often. The marquis often finds opportunities to mention his personal valet, his extraordinary good health, and his particular skill at writing letters of recommendation for various friends, habits that are "truly Roman in the worst sense of this word." At one point Montagna is about to make a statement when the public minister commands: "you will take your hand from your pocket!"

Francesco Tannoia, who claims to have been involved with Wilma in "mysterious and lucrative activities," arrives in Venice with a prepared statement of retraction. "In my capacity as a man, with all the courage I can summon, and in the full conscience of an Italian citizen, I solemnly declare that everything I wrote or said during the judicial inquiry is completely false. May the court consider the suggestiveness of the press, the cinema, and the decadent atmosphere of that period in deciding my fate."

After Tannoia, perjurer Pasquale Venuti reads his own succinct retraction: "I can guarantee that the woman [on board a car, who lost packets of white powder from her purse after hitting Venuti's motorbike] was not Wilma Montesi." President Tiberi speaks to both of these memoirists with the plural "voi" form, an ironic gesture of old-style, overly formal courtesy. In our English-language screenplay we could approximate this usage by having Tiberi use the royal "we." Whereas Tannoia blames his false testimony on the decadent Roman climate, Venuti continues to swear that at the time of the motorbike accident, he truly believed the woman he saw in the American car was Wilma Montesi, and he maintains that he was not paid by any tabloids for his story.

The Montesis return to Venice during the second week of the trial to discuss the origin of the footbath hypothesis. Contrary to the implications of the press over the four preceding years, during the trial Maria Petti herself claims full responsibility for the thesis, and she swears under oath that it *had* occurred to her before Rosa Passarelli's visit to the apartment on April 14 (after Wilma's picture was first published in the papers).

Police inspector Morlacchi explains how he first formed a *suicide* hypothesis: of all the information he received during the first few days, the inspector had been particularly struck by something Maria Petti said in passing. Once, Wilma had confessed to her mother that Giuliani "tried to lack respect for her" on a date in the Villa Borghese. Morlacchi surmised that Wilma neglected to tell the whole story to her mother, and he supposed that if the girl had indeed "lost her respect" before her marriage to Giuliani she might have attempted suicide. Moreover, Morlacchi's initial conviction was not weakened by Rosa Passarelli's subsequent declaration: "that girl did not have the look of someone who was suicidal." He was convinced that sores on Wilma's feet were an extreme disgrace for the young girl. Let us recall, however, that the first article in the *Messenger* after Wilma's body was identified, printed on April 14, mentions that after lunch on April 9, Wilma asked Wanda to go with her to Ostia *so she could send a postcard to her fiancé*. This is printed as statement of fact, not as a theory of family members. The article was not signed (although it was certainly written by journalist-lawyer Fabrizio Menghini). Did Menghini actually hear about the postcard from one of the Montesis or did he extrapolate? Does the postcard theory negate the footbath theory?

The formation of theories and the question of allegiances within the Montesi family will occupy days of testimony during the Venice trial.

A lawyer named Lemme testifies that he telephoned Wanda in 1954, offering his services to the family should they plan a civil suit.

At that time Wanda responded, "I would never bring a civil suit against Piccioni and Montagna. They are innocent. To think that in our family we didn't even know [Attilio] Piccioni was a politician. We barely knew De Gasperi and Togliatti. But if the justice system finds a criminal—if there was a criminal act—I would form a civil party, even if the guilty party were my own uncle!" When interrogated later about this statement, Wanda explains that she meant it in a generic sense, that she had not the slightest suspicion about Zio Giuseppe.

By the second week of the trial, the defense is basking in the newfound legitimacy of the footbath theory, despite the many contradictions and holes in the Montesis' stories.

The complex, contradictory testimony of the examiners and "superexaminers" of Wilma's corpse also appears to help the defense, as it moves the time of death back toward the evening of the ninth. Wilma was certainly dead by the morning of the tenth, thus discrediting any witnesses who claimed to have seen her alive that afternoon.

During lengthy and highly technical testimony by medical experts on the rictus of cadavers, a woman in the audience suddenly shouts out, "I am Wilma Montesi!" Two police officers try to restrain her as she grabs onto the drapery covering the window that faces out on the Grand Canal. As the police surround the woman, she cries: "Look at the bees coming to the honey!" A doctor in the room murmurs loudly: "A neuropath." The woman turns out to be a domestic in a wealthy Venetian household.

When confronted during the Venice trial, the Capocotta guards do little to help clear up matters. Several are illiterate and all speak with colorful Roman dialects, using expressions that often confuse court stenographers. The guards provide an amusing class spectacle, and although their stories do not add up, the contradictions seem to indicate not a cover-up but rather a different kind of logic than the one that governs the court.

○

Anna Maria Caglio arrives in Venice. She has bleached her hair blonde, and as she walks through the streets near the Rialto Bridge, a worker in coveralls thrusts a puppy into her arms. Photographers mob her. Finally the trial seems to be reaching its apex. After all, when we last heard from Caglio she was cut off as she was preparing to speak about her spiritual will. We now expect her to complete her sentence, to wipe away the tedium of the Montesis with their endless deliberations about who thought what and when. But instead, Anna Maria Caglio digresses. She recounts a plot by Piero Piccioni and Ugo Montagna to get a Roman hairdresser to bribe her with the promise of a new Alfa Romeo Giulietta, the emblematic car of Italy's economic "boom" (which is just beginning to take off).

Before a skeptical audience, Anna Maria Caglio cheerfully repeats her statements about drugs, nude suppers, and orgies at Montagna's house. She declares that Montagna kept her a virtual prisoner in his house after she tailed him and a female companion in her car. He tried to feed her poisoned spaghetti. Although these statements are certainly provocative, we've heard them all before, and they sound old hat, as if Caglio were reading from a script.

Immediately after Caglio testifies, lawyers for Montagna and Piccioni ask that the court condemn her for perjury. The request is denied—the court asserts that Caglio has to be put in confrontation with various witnesses before they can pronounce on her testimony. As Fabrizio Menghini notes in the *Messenger*, instead of trying to implicate Caglio, the defense lawyers should express their eternal gratitude to the "daughter of the century," whom they now call "giant cloud," for her vague, hackneyed stories appear nothing if not helpful to the accused.

After Caglio is excused, Zio Giuseppe is brought in to testify. The youngest of the ten children of Wilma's paternal grandfather, Riccardo Montesi, Giuseppe is an easy-

Anna Maria Caglio returns to her hotel after testifying in Venice. Expectations about her testimony ran high.

ited the apartment on Via Tagliamento during that period, perhaps because Rodolfo felt his bachelor brother was a bad influence on young Sergio. Giuseppe tells a tabloid weekly that he rarely saw his nieces. On one occasion, he and his fiancée drove Wilma and Angelo Giuliani to a dinner to introduce Giuliani to Wilma's grandparents. Giuliani and *Giuseppe's* fiancée, Mariella Spissu, got out of the car to buy cigarettes. Giuseppe then turned to his niece and said: "So you've gone and gotten engaged." Wilma replied, "Yes," in an apparently unenthusiastic tone of voice. "Well what can I do?" Giuseppe shrugged. That was the end of the conversation. In Venice, Giuseppe confirms his statement published in a tabloid that Wilma was of extremely limited intelligence. The court has nothing concrete to pursue at this point. Zio Giuseppe is dismissed and our viewers may wonder why we have bothered to show him at all.

○

President Tiberi and his colleagues determine that the court must visit Tor Vaianica in order to familiarize the magistrates with the terrain, and to personally interrogate various residents. A photograph by Velio Cioni reveals how extraordinarily bulky the judicial apparatus appears, transplanted to the otherworldly atmosphere of the beach in early spring.

In the four years since Wilma's death, the area has turned from a rather squalid and deserted beachfront, used primarily for quail hunting, into a blossoming resort with long boulevards, charming summer cottages, florescent lights, "American-style" bars, a cinema, and even a restaurant featuring "Spaghetti alla Capocotta." (When the Rome soccer team plays on the road, opposing fans yell, "Capocotta!") The regulars at Tor Vaianica—the workers and farmers who have lived there for years and witnessed this economic boom—never believed that Wilma was drowned at Ostia. Popular wisdom

The bulky appara-
tus of the court vis-
iting Tor Vaianica.

We should follow the magistrates and their entourage as they enter the main gate of
the reserve—the gate by which guests at a party might enter—and they make their
way through the interior road that leads to the sea.

**Scene from the end of *La dolce vita* when a jaded Marcello crashes through a closed gate
of an estate near the sea as he drives a group of Via Veneto habitués to Nadia's di-
vorce/striptease party.**

This was the road taken by Prince d'Assia with his companion, and it is probably the
road taken by whoever accompanied Wilma Montesi—at least, in one version of
the story. In 1953 the road that links the edge of the reserve with Ostia—the lit-
toral—was not yet finished, so a car could drive from Tor Vaianica to Capocotta,
but not from Capocotta to Ostia. Wilma's body was found about three kilometers
south of the road. The court visits a small house, just inside the gate, that according to Anna Maria Caglio was used for orgies. Jurists enter a damp room used by
the hunting society to store supplies. The house lacks a bathroom. After viewing the
"orgy house," the court makes its way onto the beach as hordes of photographers attempt every sort of acrobatics to get a view of the party. At first we might view the
scene from the paparazzi's point of view, with jerky camera motions and long shots
to suggest that we are excluded. Then we might jump-cut over to the men in overcoats walking in the sand, since even their "private" excursion is highly cinematic.

As expected, the visit yields little significant information. "The sand does not speak,"
Public Minister Palminteri comments.

Back in Venice the question of Giuseppe's whereabouts on the night of Wilma's disappearance is not resolved, as each side continues to affirm its version of events.

The court questions the portion of Giuseppe's alibi that concerns his work hours. As was
common in Italy of the 1950s, Giuseppe supplemented his main income with a second job, doing the books three afternoons a week at the Casciani plant (housed in a
sixteenth-century building where, during the height of the Counter Reformation, Saint
Filippo Neri carried out his charitable works). Giuseppe was responsible for calculat-
ing and issuing paychecks, so his hours were rather flexible, perhaps increasing toward
payday. In fact, the paychecks had to be prepared on April 9, and Giuseppe always
maintained that on that evening, given the urgency of the work, he could not possibly
have left the plant earlier than 8:30 P.M. During preliminary interviews, Giuseppe repeatedly told police they could verify his whereabouts on the evening of Wilma's disappearance by checking the signatures on the pay envelopes. His alibi seems airtight.

Called to testify on a chilly and wet morning, journalist Fabrizio Menghini, an exceptionally tall man, is forced to duck in the entranceway to the tribunal. Menghini re-

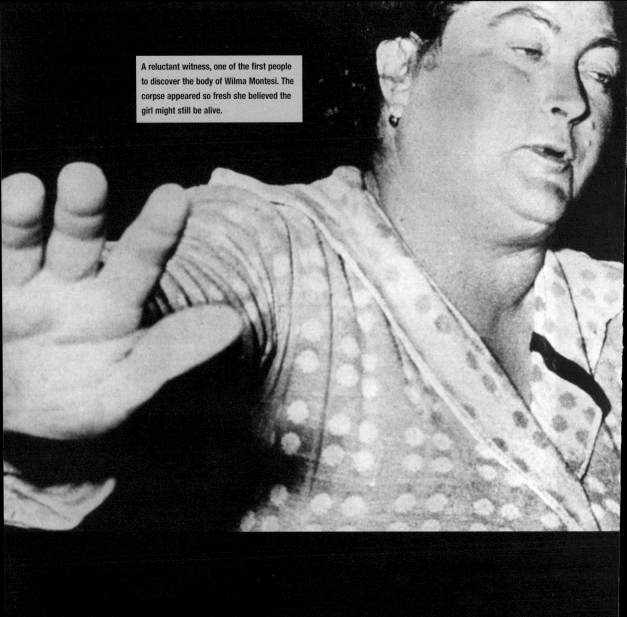

A reluctant witness, one of the first people to discover the body of Wilma Montesi. The corpse appeared so fresh she believed the girl might still be alive.

Nadia's striptease party from *La dolce vita*, held in a modern home near the sea.

mains convinced that someone—probably Zio Giuseppe—followed Wilma to the beach on April 9, 1953. After she either fainted or died—perhaps as a result of some attempted libidinal act—that person, who knew about her desire for a footbath, removed her garter belt and stockings. Menghini explains that he has always believed the Montesi family. "If Wilma did go out to parties, she must have done so with the explicit knowledge of her entire family: her sister, who slept across from her in the dining room; her brother, Sergio, whose tiny cot was in a maid's room just off the dining room; her grandmother, who slept on a folding bed in the apartment foyer; her mother, who rose before dawn every day to prepare breakfast. It is impossible to imagine that each and every member of the Montesi clan has been engaged in a massive cover-up. So I conclude that the Montesis truly believe Wilma went to bathe her feet. If any mistake was made during the investigation it was the authorities' refusal to believe the family, who expressed signs of grief and anguish as early as 9:00 P.M. when they did not have news of their daughter."

We hear testimony from Giuseppe's colleagues. When first questioned by investigators about Giuseppe's character, they had spoken favorably. They did not immediately come forward with evidence that he may have been missing from work during the critical hours of Wilma's trip to the beach. Only after several months had elapsed— enough time that one might easily forget specific details—did the plant employees seem to sour on the bookkeeper. Why? Zio Giuseppe explains, "I only know that at the time, the director of the plant was lamenting the fact that the responsibility for Wilma's death had been assigned to Piero Piccioni."

Long before Wilma's disappearance, Giuseppe had once boasted to Lionello that he had made love with a girl who was engaged to another man, but who had promised herself to Giuseppe before her marriage. In exchange, Giuseppe would buy this girl her wedding dress. When Lionello read in the papers that Wilma's uncle helped pay for the wedding dress in which his niece was buried, the plant manager began to ponder the possibility of an illicit relationship between the two.

After Giuseppe is placed in direct confrontation with his boss, Piero Piccioni's lawyer demands that the court be emptied. The public and journalists file out, shattering the dramatic tension.

During an hour-long private session before the magistrates, Giuseppe finally breaks down and confesses that he did leave work on April 9, 1953, at around 5:00 after receiving a call. The call was not from his niece, Wilma, but from Rossana Spissu, the sister of his "official fiancée." He has been having a secret affair with Rossana even though he still planned to marry her sister, Mariella! Rossana spent the morning of the ninth in Ostia. She phoned Giuseppe from a booth close to his place of work. Shortly afterward, the couple met outside the Casciani plant and drove in Giuseppe's Giardinetta to Via Flaminia, where they "parked" until dark.

After the make-out session with Rossana, Giuseppe returned home at around 11:00 P.M. So whatever time Maria Petti called his house—whether at 8:55 or 10:00 or sometime in between—Giuseppe was not there.

Silence reigns momentarily in the court. Then President Tiberi demands to know more about this secret relationship. How long had it been going on? Did anyone else know about it? Could anyone else verify this alibi?

Giuseppe explains that his "unofficial fiancée," Rossana, has given birth to a son, Riccardo, who is now two years old. Sometimes the couple met in the apartment of a friend of Rossana's in Ostia, but Giuseppe neither rented nor owned his own pied-à-terre, as he had apparently boasted to colleagues. The affair had been going on for three years.

Upon hearing this second alibi, the public minister demands that Zio Giuseppe be arrested for perjury, but President Tiberi refuses. He has another strategy in mind.

First, Ida Montesi, who has been sequestered during her brother's revelations, is recalled to the stand. Without knowing of the transformation in Giuseppe's status, she stubbornly repeats the party line, insisting that on the evening in question her brother returned from work, ate dinner, and then left to accompany his fiancée home. But under severe pressure of interrogation she begins to crack. She *thought* she was certain about details of the family dinner, but it is possible she might not recall perfectly after four years. However, Ida claims she had no idea about any relationship between her brother and Rossana Spissu. For four years Ida, Zio Giuseppe, Rossana, and Mariella have all maintained that on that fateful afternoon Giuseppe worked at the plant and returned directly home for the usual family dinner (alibi 1). Now admitting they lied, these four witnesses are discredited and are immediately dismissed. Although he might have arraigned all four on charges of false testimony, President Tiberi reserves judgment for a later date.

After the general public is readmitted to the courtroom, Zio Giuseppe suffers a dramatic fall and the tone of our film changes radically. What had begun as a trial of the privileged class is now about family squabbles and denials, petty jealousy and squalid affairs.

Over and over, Rodolfo and Maria Petti maintain that they know nothing about an affair between Giuseppe and Rossana. They offer clichéd statements about defending their family name, alternating with quips about how stupid they've always found Rossana. Wanda Montesi is recalled to the stand. She claims that she and Wilma rarely saw their uncle. They did not know that Giuseppe worked a second job in a typesetting plant, and they certainly did not have his number there. She is in her eighth month of pregnancy. Her voice and idioms strike many observers as being identical to her mother's. The Montesis all speak in proper Italian, using abstract words like "sanctity" and "decorum."

When Zio Giuseppe reveals his secret affair and the bastard son born to Rossana, the mother of Rossana and Mariella suffers a nervous collapse. She lives in a sort of temporary barracks in the Pietralata district outside of Rome, made famous by Pasolini in his postwar writings and films.

As the court considers Giuseppe's fate, he is advised to stay away from work and to avoid any contact with Rossana. Reporters besiege the Spissu family shack to no avail.

Giuseppe Montesi's supplanting of alibi 1 with alibi 2 sparks a sea change in Anna Maria Caglio's fate. Caglio has been positioned as an honest voice exposing corruption on the Right. Now as she is called back to the stand, the Venice court offers Caglio a way out of her prior testimony: "You still have time to retract various statements without consequences," says President Tiberi in a paternal tone. She declines.

Piero Piccioni remains a distant presence throughout the proceedings. He rarely appears in court, preferring to spend his afternoons at the piano. He dresses in black, and entertains few guests apart from his lawyers and his brother Leone. In contrast, a jovial Ugo Montagna is often spotted dining out in Venice. Although the public does not seem fond of either man—Piccioni is considered cold and privileged; Montagna comes off as the too-elegant Sicilian, linked with the suspicious business of real estate speculation—the "innocentists" seem to prevail.

Zio Giuseppe decides to sue two journalists who have implied that he is guilty of murder.

Flashback. Just after Wilma's funeral is breaking up, a journalist for the *European*, Luciano Doddoli, drives Giuseppe around the cemetery. Fabrizio Menghini of the *Messenger* is in the backseat, leaning forward, his head hitting the roof. Giuseppe appears extremely curious to know what the police are thinking. Doddoli baits him: "Don't you know that there are witnesses who saw you with Wilma in the car?" Giuseppe immediately responds: "Where?" Put on the spot, Doddoli hesitates before answering, "At the customs checkpoint."

"Impossible," Giuseppe answers back. "Show me the proof."

For a moment, the journalist is stymied. "Listen," says Doddoli, finally, with resolve. "There was a man in Wilma's life and let's say it once and for all: that man is you."

"Please don't use my name. For God's sake, I'll help you in any way I can, but please don't use my name," begs Giuseppe. Naturally, this response does not constitute an admission of guilt.

○

Back to the present. Our camera should pan across a small Venetian café where we see various extras reading newspapers (in English). While the headlines of the papers should announce the historic signing of the Treaties of Rome, we should make certain that our readers are passing over this news, in favor of an advertisement for a contest: "Have you formed a precise theory on the Montesi case? You can win prizes! You'll find the form and the contest rules on page two. Just fill out your name and address, send in the card, and you could win a 150 cc Vespa, a television set, a washing machine or a refrigerator!"

Traveling shot from the piazza into the courtroom, where our camera should zoom in on a plain white envelope—which seems to catch the light, like Poe's purloined letter—on the desk of court president Tiberi. Eventually, Tiberi will toy with the envelope as he becomes increasingly agitated during testimony by journalist/lawyer Fabrizio Menghini concerning his relationship with the Montesi family. A lunch recess is called and Tiberi leaves the envelope behind.

But after lunch, he finally opens the letter. After he has digested its contents, he reads it aloud to the other magistrates. The letter is from a woman named Fulvia Piastra, an old friend of the Spissu family. She writes that after hearing of Zio Giuseppe's testimony, and after much soul-searching and debate, she has come to realize her obligation to publicly announce that on the afternoon of April 9, 1953, Rossana Spissu could not have been with Zio Giuseppe. After spending the morning in Ostia, Rossana was at Termini Station in Rome to see Piastra's mother off on a train trip.

Shocked, the court immediately summons Fulvia Piastra to Venice. Meanwhile, police locate a voucher book, confirming a train trip by the elderly Signora Piastra on April 9! (Shot of public in court gasping and standing up upon hearing of this discovery.) Fulvia Piastra impresses observers as a rational and careful individual, a person with no apparent motive for intervening in the case other than to tell the truth. Her tentative rationality contrasts favorably with Rossana's fierce and emotional obduracy. She notes that several days after her mother's departure, Rossana told her, "Just think, I was arriving from Ostia as Wilma was leaving." When the court asked Piastra why she herself was interested in the disappearance of a girl whom she did not know, Piastra (again in marked contrast with many of the witnesses) explained, "I was not interested." It was Rossana who had made the connection, after Rosa Passarelli's discussion with the family placed Wilma on the 5:30 train.

As one journalist notes, it is difficult to believe that the Piastra family recalled such details after four years. On the other hand, it is difficult to imagine that they are lying. Palminteri, the public minister, defines the Piastras as "good people sent to us from Providence."

When placed in confrontation with the Piastra family, Rossana Spissu has nothing concrete to offer. She denies going to Termini Station on the day in question, although she admits accompanying Signora Piastra on other occasions. "They can say what they want," Rossana concludes, "I did not go."

The discussion continues . . .

Spissu: I swear it on my child.

P.M.: Leave your child out of this!

Spissu: He is the most beautiful thing I have in this world.

President Tiberi: We don't doubt that.

P.M.: Don't bring your child into this courtroom. Leave him at home, leave him at home!

Spissu: (crying) It cost me dearly to tell the truth, but I told it.

P.M.: It did not cost you dearly. Everyone knew already.

Spissu: I can't look my mother in the eyes . . .

P.M.: It didn't cost you anything.

Spissu: It may seem impossible to you, but the truth cost me terribly. I lost my job, I lost everything. I can't look my mother in the eyes, I can't look at my sister in the eyes, I can't look at my brother . . .

Crying, she pulls out a snapshot of the child and shows it to the court. The magistrates seem to soften, even suggesting that she is speaking under Zio Giuseppe's influence, and that her motives for lying are understandable. Although she is offered various ways out of her story, she remains obstinate even when threatened with jail, given that she does not enjoy the juridical privilege of spousal nonincrimination (this is really rubbing it in).

At this point, most people believe that even if Giuseppe was not directly involved in Wilma's death, he knows what happened to her.

Piero Piccioni and Ugo Montagna have been eclipsed.

At the same time, a letter for President Tiberi arrives from an elderly ex–parliamentary deputy and ex-editor of the satirical journal *Yellow Blackbird*. In the letter, the deputy describes his early investigations into Piccioni's possible involvement in the affair. He insists that various members of the Piccioni family offered contradictory alibis, and the influenza story only gelled after the press made ironic comments about the discrepancies. In fact, the deputy notes that it was Attilio Piccioni who had been sick, not his son. Moreover, Ugo Montagna is a close friend of the pope's personal physician and in a very good position to pull strings within the medical establishment.

On the day Fulvia Piastra causes Giuseppe's second alibi to fall apart, the public expects a confession of his guilt, or the rapid discovery of incriminating evidence. President Tiberi asks for the suspension of testimony for three weeks in order to redirect the proceedings. The trial transcripts relating to Giuseppe are placed in P.M. Palminteri's office for consideration, a request that seems to signal an impending judicial inquiry.

Giuseppe, Rossana, and Signora Spissu return to Rome, hounded by journalists. During this period, everyone associated with the case is reinterviewed, and journalists even manage to locate Adele Montesi, the fourth of the ten children of Riccardo—a sister of Rodolfo and Giuseppe, and the so-called Cinderella of the family who seems to be the only one willing to talk (apparently out of spite) to journalists after Giuseppe's confessions.

On March 25 the leaders of Europe arrive in Rome to sign the treaties of European unity, paving the way, eventually, for a common currency, the euro.

Shot of the flags of Belgium, France, West Germany, Italy, Luxembourg, and Holland flying triumphantly from the windows of the Campidoglio in Rome. The signing is broadcast on television—the first live broadcast in the history of Italian TV. We can show a television playing the ceremony in a store window in Venice. But no one is watching, because Italians are too busy following newspaper accounts of the latest testimony in the Montesi trial. We can show a classroom in which a young boy with perfectly combed hair and a neat blue smock raises his hand, stands, and asks his teacher about the future importance of the Treaties of Rome. The teacher, who has a folded copy of the *Messenger* on his desk bearing a huge Montesi headline, is at a loss to respond.

○

Wilma's ex-fiancé, Angelo Giuliani, is called to the stand. He impresses observers as particularly thickheaded, and at one point P.M. Palminteri warns him, "Try not to be any dumber than you are." In response to various questions concerning the family, Giuliani maintains a moody silence. When pressed about relations between the Montesis of Via Tagliamento and their other relatives, Giuliani states that he never took any interest; asked whether Wilma may have gone out alone in the afternoons during the period prior to her death, he replies, "It does not concern me." And when asked why the family refused to see him after the death of Wilma, he recalls: "It happened . . . and then I went away . . . There was nothing left for me to do with the Montesis."

Shot of Wilma's dresser, and untouched box with simple but elegant pearl earrings. We know Wilma told her mother and the doorkeeper that these earrings were a gift from her fiancé. Giuliani denies ever having given her earrings. If this is true, then who did give Wilma the earrings? Another man? Palminteri pushes Giuliani: "You are originally from the South, so you are a jealous type . . ." Giuliani appears not to understand the line of questioning. "Is it true," the public minister continues, "that Wilma put on two coats of lipstick to avoid being kissed?" "I kissed her a few times," Giuliani responds, nonresponsively.

After Giuliani, Sergio Montesi, now twenty years old, is called. He is questioned about his uncle, and several times he repeats the same phrase, trailing off, "I don't see how an uncle, who is of our blood . . ."

In spite of the apparent rancor within the family, the Montesis beg the court to stop persecuting Zio Giuseppe. Finally, they withdraw their civil claim against the original three defendants. Ironically, while the point of their civil case was to protect the memory of their daughter, they end up besmirching the family name. Indeed, public opinion turns against them inasmuch as they appear litigious, they are unable to furnish important details about Wilma's habits, and they doggedly defend their "blood," Zio Giuseppe, even after his two alibis collapse.

The trial is coming to an end. P.M. Palminteri's closing arguments focus on four cardinal points:

Lack of any material evidence regarding Piero Piccioni's involvement in Wilma's death

Inadmissibility of Caglio's memoirs and testimony

Lack of proof against Ugo Montagna

Lack of proof of any willful accessory on the part of Police Chief Saverio Polito

Although Palminteri notes many errors in the initial investigations, we must not forget that both the police and the carabinieri reached the same conclusion: Wilma's death was accidental, a *disgrazia*. And although Carabiniere Pompei's report on Sicilian businessman Ugo Montagna was not exactly favorable, it proved nothing regarding this particular case. As for what the report said about Polito, it tended to be rather historical in nature, focusing on the prefect's activities in the 1940s.

Palminteri also categorically dismisses the suicide hypothesis as it was first furnished by Rodolfo Montesi, and then revived by his sister Ida Montesi, after she realized her brother Giuseppe was going to be implicated. "Wilma wasn't happy with her fiancé Giuliani," the public minister continues, "and yet she did become engaged to him—to each his own—but she could have broken the engagement at any time. Economic reasons? While the Montesis weren't rich, they were comfortable. Even though there were three able-bodied women in the household (not including Wilma's grandmother), they hired a maid, that Annunziata Gionni who is, in our opinion, credible."

Although at first Gionni seemed to be exaggerating about the family's fights and peculiar animosities, in the light of Giuseppe's fall and subsequent revelations of Montesi squabbles, her remarks appear truthful. In any case, she described Wilma as a "normal" girl, and not a saint as her mother would have it.

Palminteri also notes various considerations that would seem to mitigate against Wilma's absolute sanctity: the eccentricity of a mother—Maria Petti—who, almost immediately upon her return home, began to worry about her daughter's whereabouts; who waited until her husband had taken the tram to the morgue to telephone her in-laws, for the alleged double purpose of receiving comfort (this was utterly illogical given the poor state of the relationship between the families), and of asking for a car (also illogical, given that her husband, the only member of the family with a driver's license, had already left the house via public transportation); who arrived at the cemetery to view her daughter's headstone sporting a "slutty" hairstyle.

Palminteri concludes that Wanda is also hiding something.

The sentence pronounced by Tiberi grants full absolution to Piccioni (for not having committed the crime) and to Montagna and Polito. Piccioni's sentence leaves open the possibility that a crime may indeed have been committed (by another individual). By absolving Piccioni, the court logically presumes that the crimes of accessory charged to Montagna and Polito were not valid. Finally, the Venice tribunal ends up contradicting the police and carabinieri, and confirming Raffaele Sepe's conclusions in the judicial inquiry that Wilma's death was not a *disgrazia*, but caused by slow drowning at Tor Vaianica, not Ostia. Palminteri appears particularly dismissive of the footbath hypothesis, saying it was clear that Wilma would not have gone out so late on a stormy day, and that she would not have been able to reach the station in time to take the train at 5:30.

The colorful Capocotta guards are also acquitted for lack of any crime; tabloidist Mercedes Borgatti is pardoned; the "drug traffickers" are acquitted of false testimony upon retraction of their original statements; and former stenographer Adriana Bisaccia, virtually erased from public memory, is sentenced to ten months' imprisonment and subject to court costs and fines. Her prison term will later be converted to probation.

As the sentence is read, Piccioni, Montagna, and Polito remain pale, with fixed expressions. Leone Piccioni rises first and embraces his brother. Then the lawyers are given time to respond to the verdict. Piccioni's defender, Carnelutti, remarks that in his opinion, much of the blame for the trial lies with the Jesuit father Dall'Olio, who first encouraged Caglio to speak out as the "moral voice" of the country. Perhaps, Carnelutti suggests, Dall'Olio had little experience with women and found himself seduced by the vivacious girl in the camel-hair coat. The fact is that after she became his protectee, she gained immense credibility, as if she were defended by the entire Society of Jesus.

Shot of Montagna and Polito leaving Venice immediately after the verdict.

Shot of Piero and Leone Piccioni at La Fenice Theater in Venice, watching Olivier in *Titus Andronicus*. (Someone has anonymously sent them two tickets for this sold-out premiere.)

The following morning Piccioni makes the seven-hour train trip back home just in time to catch Ella Fitzgerald in *The Negress*. Talking to reporters, Piccioni describes his emotions: "Do you have any idea what it means to be accused? I once read in a weekly magazine that because I had played in Harlem, with a black jazz orchestra, I must have taken on the habits shared by many blacks for taking drugs. Aside from the fact that this supposition is false, can you tell me why they would write something like this?"

Our movie could end here. We would be suspicious of Zio Giuseppe, indignant about Caglio. We would have virtually forgotten about Piero Piccioni and Ugo Montagna and so would harbor them no particular ill will. We would leave the theater disappointed that no culprit had been punished, and were we so inclined, we would recommend Wilma Montesi's soul to heaven. . . .

PART FIVE

*The Afterlife
of Scandal*

On June 6, 1957, a judge is named for a judicial inquiry against Zio Giuseppe. Two days later, he is issued an arrest warrant for libeling his former colleagues at the Casciani printing plant. We should recall that he accused *them* of lying and covering up for powerful figures when they said he left work early on the day of Wilma's death. At 11:30 A.M. several police drive to Zio Giuseppe's current office at the Ministry of the Treasury, only to learn that he has left work to attend to an urgent matter. The officers soon learn that this "urgent matter" is a double date at the beach at Anzio with another colleague and two young girls. The couples are discovered eating at the Gambero restaurant (a fixed menu of fish soup, fritto misto, fresh strawberries [in season] and coffee). The officers eavesdrop as Zio Giuseppe makes a phone call, and they hear him exclaim, "Yes *avvocato*, I'll come to Rome immediately!" He is stopped in a Fiat 1100 on his way to the offices of his lawyer near the Vatican. By 5:00 P.M. he is locked in solitary confinement.

In theory, a charge of libel should not carry a prison sentence, but the magistrates want to make sure Giuseppe is out of the way while they carry on with their investigation.

Rossana Spissu, the mother of Giuseppe's child, is also charged, with false testimony. She is given probation.

Shots of tourists in shorts flocking around the Spanish Steps in the center of Rome.

In July, journalist-detective Luciano Doddoli writes an article stating that Zio Giuseppe and Zia Ida may have used both Wilma and Wanda as lookouts to help them with drug deals, without their father's knowledge. Rodolfo and Wanda decide to sue Doddoli for libel, but, oddly enough, Giuseppe and Ida refuse to join the suit. Since Doddoli's article is hardest on Giuseppe and Ida, the idea that they would not press charges appears suspicious and suggests that there are still great rifts within the family.

Around this time, President Tiberi of the Venice court becomes seriously ill and announces he will be unable to complete the *motivazione* (a lengthy document in which the court president details the findings that led to a verdict) on deadline. In the meantime, the Montesis of Via Tagliamento are questioned over and over about Zio Giuseppe and about their initial suicide hypothesis. Our viewers are growing weary of the same themes rehashed.

Finally, after serving a full ninety-seven days (!) on charges that appear to many observers as trumped-up, Giuseppe is released from prison on September 14, 1957. We should show him visibly altered by the experience. He embraces fellow prisoners as he is let free.

In early October, Tiberi finally completes his findings for the Venice trial, explaining the basis for the verdict primarily in the shiftiness of various witnesses against Piccioni; the megalomaniacal nature of fortune-teller Natalino Del Duca's ravings; and the fact that no one could verify whether Alida Valli said, "Did you know her?" or "So, you did know her!" on the phone from Venice.

Less than a week after the findings are submitted, the attorney general of Italy interrupts the judicial inquiry against Zio Giuseppe and demands the files be turned over to his office for consideration. Why? Even Zio Giuseppe's lawyers are at a loss to explain this decision, or the fact that their client has been let off the hook. Is it possible that the two magistrates in charge of the inquiry actually believe the suicide hypothesis in spite of Sepe's earlier inquiry and the Venice trial? Could these two magistrates have been swayed by the publication of the findings with their insistence on a *disgrazia*?

For the rest of the year nothing more is heard concerning Giuseppe's fate or the suspended inquiry. The newspapers drop the story. Public interest in the death of Wilma Montesi has ebbed away to a tiny stream. We can indicate this trailing off of activity by showing the various protagonists of the case "getting on with their lives." Close-up of the Zio Giuseppe inquiry papers sitting on a desk. The window is open, and a breeze blows open various files. Cut to various magistrates associated with the case discussing the latest soccer results as they drink coffee in a nearby bar.

May 1959. Six years after Wilma's death, Anna Maria Caglio reappears in a Roman court to answer to charges of aggravated slander against Montagna, Piccioni, and a hairdresser who allegedly tried to bribe Caglio with a Giulietta. She is also charged with false testimony during three distinct phases of the Montesi case: Silvano Muto's libel trial, Raffaele Sepe's judicial inquiry, and the Venice trial. Arriving at the Ugly Palace in a summery dress, her black hair cut extremely short, Anna Maria appears happy to find herself among photographers and reporters once again. The building is surrounded by a notable presence of armed officers.

Anna Maria sticks to her old stories and notes that the whole scandal would not have erupted had the *European* refrained from publishing her private spiritual will.

Shot of Anna Maria Caglio testifying, intercut with shots of elderly Saverio Polito taking his last breath and being covered with a sheet as a priest performs the last rites.

The court grants parole to Anna Maria Caglio.

⟲

Several months pass. Shots of tourists crowding the Via Veneto in Rome. Jaded regulars honk impatiently in the traffic.

⟲

August 1959. Zio Giuseppe is again charged with aggravated slander by his four ex-colleagues at the Casciani printing plant. We must recall that he already spent more than three months in prison for similar charges.

Simultaneously, Rossana Spissu, the mother of his child, is accused of giving false testimony in Venice. Their trials will not begin for nearly a year.

A throng of reporters bangs on the Spissu shack until finally, exasperated, Rossana's mother opens the creaky door, fashioned from corrugated metal. As reporters yell out questions, Signora Spissu begs, "Leave us alone. Please! Every family has problems, and we have the right to keep them to ourselves. Why are we forced to hang our dirty laundry in public? It isn't fair. We don't want publicity." Pan over to a makeshift communal clothesline in the center of the group of shacks, held up by stakes driven into the muddy ground. Dirty laundry flaps in the breeze.

⟲

May 1960. Anna Maria Caglio gets married. Since the Venice trial, she has been painting and has even worked briefly as a photojournalist, living between Florence and Rome. She meets a university student/businessman/noted nightclubber named Mario Ricci through mutual friends. They dance in a famous bar on the Via Veneto, and two days later, Ricci asks for Anna Maria's hand, saying that her past does not interest him.

The marriage takes place three weeks later. Cars of reporters tail the couple as they leave the groom's home in Forte dei Marmi and head for Florence, but the couple manages to lose them. A photojournalist from a tabloid weekly has paid two and a half million lire for the exclusive rights to photograph the ceremony. Caglio has also promised the weekly a new "memoir" on her marriage to accompany the images. All the other reporters imagine that Caglio is planning to get married in some small, private chapel, and no one suspects that she will choose the traditional Santissima Annunziata, where many couples, even if they marry elsewhere, come to spread orange blossoms on the altar of the Madonna according to an old custom.

In the chapel are works by the Renaissance and Baroque painters Vasari, Pontormo, and Andrea del Sarto. Caglio does not bother with the orange blossoms.

Bridegroom Ricci is dressed in a subdued gray suit; Caglio in a light Nile-blue dress. She has forgotten her hat. Someone scurries to find a veil.

This is the last time we will see Anna Maria Caglio on film. We might say that during the course of our screenplay, she has matured. She has settled down. She no longer clamors for attention, but is content to live her life as an Anygirl. But to arrive at this conclusion is to ignore a profound fact of Everyday Life in the Modern World: in her extreme behavior, Anna Maria has taught us that all subjects in the Modern World, to some degree, are acting in front of a perpetual camera, whether motion-picture or still. Most subjects are not normally conscious of the presence of the camera, or they have internalized it. Anna Maria has often looked directly into its lens, and she has flirted with her public. In doing so, she has only made manifest what seems to be a deeply buried, perhaps dirty secret: that we all live filmed or photographed lives, a condition made both possible and necessary in Italy by the postwar developments of rosy neorealism, documentary film, and paparazzi.

November 1960. Magistrates prepare to hear the trial against Zio Giuseppe and Rossana Spissu. For some time now, Giuseppe has not worked as an accountant, but is instead a salesman for a toilet company. The plaintiffs in the case are the four workers from the Casciani plant named by Giuseppe in *his* earlier suit. In order to show that *Giuseppe* did not slander his colleagues by suing *them* after *they* said he might have been involved in Wilma's death, the defense must prove not only that Zio Giuseppe did *not* go to Ostia on April 9, 1953, but that he never met up with his niece Wilma. After so many years, this seems impossible. The trial is held in one of the largest courtrooms in Rome to accommodate a crowd of journalists and witnesses.

Rossana Spissu has been offered amnesty, but she refuses, once again, to change her story. She continues to affirm that on the ninth of April, 1953, she and Giuseppe took a drive. She did not go to the station that day with the Piastra family. They must have remembered the event incorrectly.

The Casciani workers repeat information we have already heard in some form or another. At such a great distance, the recounting of times, dates, and apparently minor facts about Giuseppe's behavior seems disingenuous. We should note the tedium of this testimony by showing reporters yawning at the back of the court.

The Montesis of Via Tagliamento continue to deny any possibility of an affair between Wilma and the uncle she had met only a handful of times in her adult life. Other witnesses confirm their prior testimony. Wilma's maternal grandmother is called to the stand. She supports the footbath theory, which she claims she heard in the house just after Wilma's disappearance.

In the meantime, the train voucher booklet used by Fulvia Piastra's mother has gone missing from among the documents entered into evidence in Venice. Perhaps, a court official notes, it was transferred to Rome along with other papers in the slander trial of Anna Maria Caglio.

Who started all the rumors about Zio Giuseppe? The court determines that the original "Operation Giuseppe" was organized, in part, by Signor Biagetti of the printing plant, who was a vague acquaintance of Piero Piccioni. However, it was not logical that Zio Giuseppe's colleague would have initiated a witch hunt in order to help a vague acquaintance, no matter how strong his political allegiances. Yes, Biagetti did turn to the authorities on the day following Piccioni's arrest, but only because the event sparked his memory. The evidence about the origin of accusations against Giuseppe is inconclusive.

It is time for the verdict. According to the public minister, Wilma was a girl of "irresistible ambition" who "knew what she wanted: she had decided to rise above the condition of a modest carpenter; she was fascinated by cars, those great temptations of modern civilization. Wilma's father, Rodolfo, had possessed a car for a short time; but business was bad and he had to get rid of it. Wilma never forgave him for this. As a typical girl [we might say, an Anygirl], the car represented, for her, the most powerful of dreams because it would set her apart from her friends and from the other tenants of her building. In this context, she got to know her Zio Giuseppe. . . . He was handsome, a real seducer; but above all, he owned a car." The public minister asks for a sentence of two years and two months for Giuseppe on the slander charges. Rossana Spissu is also sentenced to a short jail term for her false testimony.

Giuseppe and Rossana leave the court in Giuseppe's new car, a white station wagon. The pair drive to the Verano cemetery and leave yellow chrysanthemums on the tomb of Wilma Montesi. After a moment of silence, they depart. Later Giuseppe and Rossana will appeal their sentences.

February 1963. Nearly ten years after Wilma's death, Zio Giuseppe and Rossana Spissu await word on their appeals of their sentences. The court decides to absolve Giuseppe of aggravated slander and Rossana of false testimony. Observers understand that with this judgment, the court implicitly clears Giuseppe of any presumed involvement in the death of his niece, and puts an end to any further investigations into the matter. Giuseppe may now leave his toilets and return to his old job as an accountant for the state, should he so desire. In the last year, Giuseppe has finally married Rossana, who attends the hearing in a late stage of pregnancy. Rossana, in tears, approaches the bench and says, "May God bless you." At this point, even Zio Giuseppe cannot hold back his tears. The courtroom is deserted and as they exit into the sunlight, they look around, perhaps almost disappointed to find no paparazzi, no frantic reporters. The absolute quiet of the piazza is shattered only by the horn of a passing Vespa.

Title: The End (over shot of Zio Giuseppe and Rossana searching for reporters in deserted piazza).

As viewers weaned on Hollywood, Zio Giuseppe and Rossana expect a greater degree of closure, perhaps even a big final song and dance number featuring all the protagonists. Such a flourish might have appealed to Wilma. (Shot of the naive Sandra in Fellini's 1953 *I vitelloni* saying, "I prefer musicals.") Our film must make clear the disparity between the expectations of the cinematized subject and lack of any juridical resolution to the case. We must signify and respect this lack, but we also have a responsibility to at least point to the implications of various positions.

We might employ the old trick of finishing with elderly versions of the protagonists, who continue to uphold their sides of the story to this day. One representative from the Right (a Mario Scelba; or even a minor figure from the case; or a journalist or scholar) with creaky voice, stating: "In all likelihood, there was some evidence to suggest that Zio Giuseppe was involved with his niece's death. At the very least, he had some idea of what happened. But by the time this evidence came to light, people were already talking about Piero Piccioni. And that suited Amintore Fanfani—representing the left wing of the Christian Democrats—just fine. To say nothing of the Left itself . . . So nothing was done, and the whole thing was allowed to get out of hand."

And one representative from the Left: "To think that such cover-ups could take place in a modern, democratic Italy. And don't think it couldn't happen again."

And so, two positions: the commonsense Right, a bit of titillation, a flirtation with incest, followed by a will to normalcy, a drive to produce; and on the Left, mild paranoia, the pleasure of conspiracy, the constancy of crisis.

Or our ending credits might reproduce an actual photoessay that appeared on the pages of *Today* magazine: "The Last Views of Wilma Montesi." It may be important to remind our viewer about Wilma, who has been neglected throughout most of our screenplay. This essay provides a summational link between magazine photography and the train departures in the actuality films of the Lumière brothers and other early cinematographers. Over several pages, the magazine printed still shots following a path from Wilma's bed to the courtyard of Via Tagliamento 76; to the street; from the window of the tram; the ticket window of the San Paolo station; ending with a POV shot from the window of the train to Ostia as it crossed the Rome city limits. Then the essay ends, as if the camera itself could not venture beyond this point of no return. The sequence of these photographs gives the sense of an increasingly widening circle of walls, protecting the city of Rome. The images are surrounded by a quasi-sacred aura, perhaps unconsciously suggesting the very ancient urban codes that still underlie the modern city. Rome consisted of an *urbs* and the rural territory attached to the city, the *ager romanus*. The circumference of the city was defined by the *pomerium*, the *post murum*, marked by furrows made by a plough and a white sow that Virgil cites in the *Aeneid* as the symbolic guarantor of the authentic ground. The city walls describe a sacred orbit, and from them the *urbs* derived its supernatural protection. Roma was believed free from defilement by foreign cults. The dead were buried outside the walls. Taboos protected the inhabitants inside.

As a backdrop for our credits, these photo essay stills would give the impression that the girl lived her short life as a camera, taking snapshots strung together with minimal continuity. Her end comes abruptly when the camera refuses to leave Rome proper. It is more comfortable—protected by ancient cults—in the center and rarely takes the trouble to venture to the periphery.

But if we wish to reproduce as faithfully as possible the cinematic contradictions of the Montesi scandal, we will simply leave Zio Giuseppe and Rossana in the piazza, in the glare of everyday life.

OUTTAKES

The following "scenes" may have to remain on the cutting room floor, either because
they are too complex or too uncinematic to be included in the final version of our
film.

Cronaca: We might wish for our viewers to grasp the significance of this term, which
refers to an item of news, most commonly published as short reportage on the
fourth pages of the newspapers. In postwar Italy, the term bears a particular tinge.
It expresses a desire for freedom. *Cronaca* can be a brief and dispensable item of
human interest, or a more lengthy narrative, but above all it must be coded as "honest" and "post-Fascist." The *cronaca* is not necessarily political in an overt sense. Instead, it reflects (and supports) a commonsense middle ground. Let us examine the
question of journalistic ideology in greater detail: like so many papers in postwar
Italy, *Il messaggero di Roma* (the *Messenger*—a key paper for the Montesi case), was
resolutely centrist. Mario Missiroli, director of *Il messaggero* beginning in 1946, was
an extremely influential figure in postwar Italian journalism, an exemplar of what
Italians call the "pastone" or opportunist. As a Christian Democrat, he oriented his
paper in the direction of centrist De Gasperi (as opposed to expressing a blind loy-
alty to the party as a whole, which he felt was in danger of moving too far to the
Right). Missiroli stayed on until 1952, when he went to become director of the Milanese paper *Corriere della sera*. In 1953, *Il messaggero* supported Attilio Piccioni as
the rightful heir to De Gasperi. On the other hand, the new director of the paper,
Alessandro Perrone, also threw his energies into reporting on the scandalistic side
of the Montesi case. It would be difficult to represent the ideology of the *cronaca*
on film. We could shoot a series of scenes in which fresh-faced young journalists
tear up Fascist propaganda and then head out with their pads and pencils to catch
a scoop. In another scene we might film a wealthy director of an unnamed paper

meeting up with various politicians in a bar near the Quirinale. The director pats the politicians on the back and calls them by first names. "Let me treat you," insists a politician, offering the paper's director a coffee. We cannot tell from any outward signs if he is from the Right or the Left.

○

Legge Truffa ("swindler's law"): The law passed to (potentially) allow the Christian Democrats to win "bonus seats" in Parliament with a majority was called the "swindler's law" by opponents. It is important, although highly uncinematic, to document the political maneuvering that may or not have directly influenced the developments of the Montesi scandal. Let us review some dates:

April 9, 1953. Wilma Montesi goes out.

April 11, 1953. Body of Wilma Montesi discovered.

June 6, 1953. Elections held. Very high voter turnout. Christian Democrats win 40.7% majority in Senate; Communists win 20.9%. In the House, the "center" wins 49.8%, while the opposition (including the extreme Left and extreme Right) wins 50.2%. This election was seen as a disaster for the Christian Democrats, in that if the center had only managed to muster 50%, they would have been entitled to bonus seats, further consolidating their power against the "extremes." Instead, voters expressed a clear dissatisfaction with the ruling party. Even the strong political influence of the Catholic Church and the vocal support of American ambassador Clare Booth Luce could not help the Christian Democrats in their quest for a majority.

The question of when Piero Piccioni's name started to circulate is crucial to the failure of the swindler's law to achieve its political ends.

There is another peculiar twist that links the law to the Montesi case. Anna Maria Caglio wrote in her memoir that Ugo Montagna once told her, "You know, we met in my house and we found the right law for the Italian people, who aren't worthy of a true democracy. We'll make it come to pass in the next elections." In fact, it was this line which really caused Amintore Fanfani to bristle and demand that a full investigation of Montagna be turned over to the carabinieri.

The Christian Democrats' failure to gain a majority had political implications for years to come.

July 2, 1953. Following election debacle, old guardsman De Gasperi is named, once again, to head government.

Several days later, Piero Piccioni withdraws suit against two left-wing journalists from

Paese sera who gave credibility to rumors surrounding his involvement in Wilma's death.

July 16. De Gasperi announces cabinet, naming himself as both president of the Council of Ministers and as foreign minister (this was not an uncommon combination); Attilio Piccioni as vice president; and Amintore Fanfani as minister of the Interior. All of the ministers in this proposed cabinet are Christian Democrats. The Left is outraged at the lack of representation outside the ruling party.

August 3. President Einaudi concludes that De Gasperi's new government is too rigid and will fail to gain consensus. He appoints Attilio Piccioni to form a government, while De Gasperi leaves for vacation in the mountains. He will never again head the government. The following summer, at age 73, he will pass away, the last of a generation.

August 13. Einaudi dismisses Attilio Piccioni and asks Pella, representing the right wing of the party, to form a new government.

August 17. Pella issues his list, excluding Piccioni entirely. Why? The Montesi scandal is never mentioned by party members. Instead, they suggest that Piccioni is simply too closely identified with De Gasperi. Fanfani is named minister of the Interior. A vote of confidence passes, the Christian Democrat Party (still officially led by De Gasperi) pledges its full support to Pella and everyone leaves for the traditional August vacation.

January 1, 1954. Without opening a government "crisis," party leader De Gasperi presents a new list of ministers to President Einaudi. The political climate has changed little since Pella's formation of a new government in August.

○

Minister Tupini, whose son, accused of dealing cocaine, will appear in a lineup for Adriana Bisaccia, resigns from public life. The usual voices crying scandal are silenced by Tupini's resolute statement that he is simply too old. Although he vows that he will never again speak to the press, Tupini finds himself besieged by reporters after the Socialist paper (and former training ground of Mussolini) *Avanti!* publishes an article stating when Piero Piccioni's involvement in the Montesi case was divulged, the then undersecretary of information (Tupini himself) took charge of a press cover-up.

January 3, 1954. Italian television begins regular programming for four hours per day. Pope Pius XII speaks of his desire that television be used to spread Christian values.

January 5. The second Montesi investigation is concluded with a verdict of *"disgrazia,"* just like the first investigation.

January 6. Pella presents President Einaudi with a list of dismissals from the government. The libel trial of Silvano Muto is postponed because the defendant is ill.

January 13. Fanfani, representing the left wing of the Christian Democrats, is named to head the government. Fanfani's new list of ministers are all members of his party, including Piccioni as foreign minister.

January 17. The Social Democrats announce they do not intend to grant Fanfani a vote of confidence, so he will have to proceed in the formation of a new government without any preestablished majority. During the turbulent moments of the vote, Fanfani yells at the members of the Communist Party because their leader, Palmiro Togliatti, had accused him of wearing the "Fascist hat."

Fanfani: Yes, I did wear it once, while recently I was able to observe a photo of the "best" of the Italian Communists with the fur hat of the Cossacks of old!

Pajetta (Communist Party): But you were a Fascist!

Fanfani: Just like you!

January 28. The Muto trial is postponed until March.

January 30. Fanfani's government (formed without Piccioni) is defeated by a vote of no confidence.

February 1954. Debates continue in Parliament, and the first signed article on the Montesi case (by Fabrizio Menghini) appears in the *Messenger* with the headline: "Anna Maria Caglio Knows How Wilma Montesi Died." With this turn of events, the case leaves the *cronaca* and becomes a matter of front-page news. Menghini's article is also graced by a photograph of Caglio reciting a vanity role in a Pirandello play.

February 9. Mario Scelba (one of Montagna's "friends") is named to head a new government. President Einaudi gives Scelba the explicit instruction that he must include members of all four "democratic" parties on his list. Scelba names Attilio Piccioni to his former post as foreign minister. Fanfani is not included. Scelba's government receives a vote of confidence at the end of February. This election is crucial inasmuch as Scelba and Fanfani are understood to represent two possible successors to De Gasperi. The right wing of the party wins the struggle, setting the course for years to come. Fanfani makes an unsuccessful bid to become secretary of the Christian Democrat Party, a post that had been previously held by

Spataro, the ex–postmaster general under De Gasperi, and another "friend" of Ugo Montagna.

March 16. Chief of Police Pavone retires.

July 1. Minister De Caro presents Parliament with his report (prepared with the help of a carabiniere investigation) on Ugo Montagna and possible dealings with other highly placed leaders. As we know, the report is inconclusive.

September 7. Magistrate Raffaele Sepe orders the seizure of the passports of Piero Piccioni, Ugo Montagna, Saverio Polito (Rome chief of police), and Prince Maurizio d'Assia.

September 18. Attilio Piccioni resigns as foreign minister, replaced by Gaetano Martino. Whereas Piccioni had straddled the fence about signing the Treaties of Rome, Martino sees that final arrangements go smoothly, and, in 1955, he leads Italy into the United Nations. Piccioni will return to political life after the conclusion of the scandal.

September 21. Piero Piccioni is arrested, along with Montagna and Polito.

November 15. A scandal explodes when noted Commie Giuseppe Sotgiu is accused of running a male prostitution ring with his wife. Four days later, Piccioni and Montagna are released from jail.

Around this time, the Italian tax code undergoes serious reforms as part of a broad moralizing of daily life. A "freelancer" like Ugo Montagna has to pay much more than before the scandal. Piero Piccioni, who had never declared any income, is finally on the tax rolls.

May 1958. We could indicate that the Montesi scandal has slipped out of collective consciousness by filming the protagonists of the case sitting on various park benches and feeding bread crumbs to pigeons. Elections are held, and without any scandals or accusations of swindling the Christian Democrats solidify the power base that they will enjoy for years to come.

March 1960. Attilio Piccioni is again asked to form a new government, but he refuses the responsibility for personal reasons. Although this response is predictable, Piccioni is still considered one of the "men of honor" of the party and is an ideal compromise candidate with the other centrist parties. One columnist describes Piccioni as a "fiancé of power who has taken a vow of chastity." In his past, Piccioni was never a hard worker. He preferred to read the classics of Italian literature, ignoring modernist and avant-garde authors altogether. A bourgeois gentleman who opposed

Fascism on moral grounds, but without fighting it, Piccioni was almost guaranteed to refuse to expose himself to another round of political fighting.

Police. At the start, the case is being investigated, and will continue to be investigated, by both the civil police and the more elite carabinieri who work directly under the auspices of the Ministry of Defense (like Rosa Passarelli, the witness who offered the family a possible account of Wilma's accidental demise). Ultimately, both police branches are responsible to the Ministry of the Interior. It is common in Italy for the two branches of the police to form different theories of a crime, and the balance of power between the two can be a delicate matter. The civil police operated in 1953 under the control of the Rome prefect, Saverio Polito. He, in turn, reported to Italy's chief of police, Tommaso Pavone, also stationed in the capital. Pavone is also an employee of the Interior. At the time of Wilma's death, that branch is led by Mario Scelba, to the far right of the political spectrum (and a friend of defendant Ugo Montagna). As noted above, Scelba will be selected as prime minister less than a year after Wilma's death.

Scandal. In Italy at this time the Right often accuses the Left of using scandal as a primary political weapon, and, in fact, Communist Party leader Togliatti insists that his party should exploit a scandal should one erupt, using morals against the party of morality. An article published in the journal *Rinascita*, edited by Togliatti, notes that while scandals have existed since the beginning of history, Fascism opened up the possibility for a new type of scandal, one in which information and evidence is manipulated for political ends. The Montesi scandal was rendered possible because of the continuity of Fascism in the rivalries of the new "bourgeois political parties" and hidden internal struggles for key posts that rarely leak to the public as they do in the Kremlin. The Montesi scandal directly forced the president of the Council of Ministers, Scelba, to address Parliament on the necessity of "moralizing daily life," noting that "government and bureaucracy exist in the service of the state; we are and we must, for this reason, in exercising our functions, remain above and beyond the parties, and the bureaucracy must be able to resist any suggestions from the political forces in order to fulfill its sole duty, to the state." Scelba admitted that many of the bureaucrats could boast of pasts filled with dubious acts. "We must recall, however, that the war and postwar periods are now over, and it is necessary to normalize the life of the state, bringing its organs under the law, eliminating all that might have been temporarily justified as a consequence of war. Governments come and go, the parties fluctuate in their power, but functionaries represent the continuity of the state and they constitute its very backbone."

Responding to the investigative committee set in motion by Scelba, and presided over by Christian Democrat minister De Caro, Communist leader Palmiro Togliatti demands that the Montesi case lead to radical changes in both domestic and foreign policies. Togliatti places little value in De Caro's "neutral" investigation, which sets several specific goals: (1) to investigate the activities of the ex–police chief, Pavone, and his possible relations with Ugo Montagna in the death of Wilma Montesi; (2) to determine if Montagna profited in the most general sense from relations with political figures; and (3) to determine if the first two investigations of Montesi's death had been performed properly or if evidence had been tainted. While the Left discredits these goals and notes that De Caro's commission never interviewed key witnesses like Anna Maria Caglio, the Christian Democrats make clear that commission must remain completely separate from the juridical proceedings, and can only have as its goal the gathering of information in the service of governmental orientation or restructuring norms for the moralization of public life or of the organs of the state.

Scelba explains in an almost pedagogical fashion that although he seeks the truth in Wilma Montesi's death, the legislative branch cannot intervene in the judicial system in a democracy; instead, it must inform its citizens of its duty to maintain the separation of powers. De Caro's commission presents its function of maintaining this separation as if "for the first time"—that is, to found the democratic regime in Italy. In fact, the public is extremely disappointed by De Caro's final draft, which reads like a tax report and avoids any suggestion of scandal. De Caro concludes that the friendship between Ministers Spataro and Piccioni was limited to their sons; that Minister Scelba and Montagna only met at the wedding of Spataro's son; that Montagna's title was valid, having been awarded in 1946 just before the monarchy was voted out of existence; that at worst, Italian police chief Pavone was guilty of failing to warn other government officials from developing friendships with Montagna, who had a criminal record and suspect business dealings.

De Caro's commission finds that all procedures were followed to the letter and that government authorities could not find any legitimate reason to reopen the Montesi case. These directives came at a time and context in which Parliament was considering a variety of regulations meant to "moralize" public life and to erase the taint of corruption associated with the Fascists. "All in all, these directives are meant to regulate, with a more rigorous discipline, an area, that, with the growing powers of the state, had been left up to chance or regulated by antiquated laws, and does not correspond to the needs of the newly formed, more complex functions entrusted to public administration."

The Left responds critically to these directives. Accusations are made that the Christian Democrats were attempting to suffocate the scandal and that De Caro's commission, with its own self-imposed limitations, simply could not go far enough in investigating the Montesi case. Meanwhile, the Christian Democrat minister, Saragat, cries out that the Montesi scandal is a totalitarian invention of the Left and the extreme Right. "It is the responsibility of the democrats [i.e., Christian Democrats] to unmask this frightening technique which destroys all values of justice and truth," Saragat notes, while a leader of the Republican Party concurs, "By making of each blade of grass a sheath [*un fascio*, the symbol of Fascism], the Communists hope to compromise as many citizens as possible along with the best qualified members of the ruling political class."

Ugo Montagna (and friends) on film. It could be useful to reveal to our viewers the long history of Ugo Montagna on the wrong side of the law, and we might do so through a snappy series of flashbacks. He is first arrested for a traffic accident in 1935 in Palermo and is ordered to return home to his small town (the Fascists were fond of issuing writs of obligatory deportation and repatriation); in 1936, Montagna is arrested in Rome for fraudulent declaration of bankruptcy in a business affair; in 1937 he is granted amnesty after charges he used fraudulent business cards; in 1941, police issue a citation after his all-night parties disturb neighbors. Montagna had married in 1936, but he was soon estranged from his wife. During the early 1940s Montagna is known for organizing "nights of pleasure" for various political figures, including German officials and Nazi civilians. Around this time the chief of police warns Montagna to avoid seeing Mussolini's children. Of the various members of Mussolini's hierarchy, Montagna was particularly close with the minister of racial affairs, whom he often invited to his country estate. He was also known in Jewish circles as one who was willing to obtain racial discrimination papers for payment. With the Liberation of Rome, Montagna soon developed close relations with American and English soldiers while he was simultaneously accused of spying for the Germans.

In 1950, Montagna and his estranged wife travel to Austria to annul their marriage. The motive given by the couple is that the wife had been mentally disturbed at the time of the wedding. But the annulment is contested by the Italian courts, and so, from a legal standpoint, the two are still officially married at the time of the Montesi scandal.

Mussolini may have made the trains run on time, but Montagna is able to stop them. One afternoon Caglio is supposed to return to Rome from Milan with her lover, but for some reason she wants to stay behind. The pair has an appointment to meet at the station at a certain time, but Caglio arrives late, on purpose. Nevertheless, Montagna is able to delay the departure of the "rapido," forcing Caglio to make the trip after all. "In Italy it is not the ministers, the great dignitaries of the state who can effect such things, but, precisely, the Montagnas: these strange people who live at the margins of power: friends in equal measure of 'his Excellency' and the station master." Caglio never understands how Montagna makes his money, but he always seems to have plenty of it.

During the height of the scandal some people question the legitimacy of Montagna's title, but investigators conclude that he has a right to call himself the marquis of San Bartolomeo, although no other member of his family had bothered to adorn themselves in a similar fashion.

Scene in which Colonel Pompei of the carabinieri takes notes while Anna Maria Caglio prattles. He then reads back his notes, which say: "Mussolini . . . Petacci [Clara Petacci was Mussolini's long-term lover; she was assassinated, strung upside down alongside il Duce] was a friend of Ugo's and he told me about black [i.e. Fascist] parties that took place in her house. Once Mussolini discovered the two of them in bed together but didn't do anything because he was afraid of Montagna. . . . The day the war broke out, June 10 [1940], Giorgio Natili [one of Montagna's close business associates in real estate] celebrated with Bruno, Vittorio [sons of il Duce] and three other men. Eighteen girls and six men, on Via Rabirio. . . . Right after the war Ugo and Mastrobuono [a government official and friend of Montagna] were involved in sugar trading (or so he said). . . . It is difficult to understand how the son of a washerwoman could make so much money in sugar; he went to Switzerland with Mastrobuono in a car with diplomatic plates belonging to the secretary general of Afghanistan. . . . Polito is a good friend of Ugo's and one day he went to lunch with Ugo and another bigwig, I forget who. Polito recounted how he had closed down a sort of . . . den of pederasts and drug pushers. He had the list of the names of bigwigs involved. Ugo explained to me that Polito wanted some kind of nice incentive to keep the names secret."

During the libel trial, Silvano Muto's lawyer, Sotgiu, asks Caglio about her first meeting with Montagna: "When he made the introduction, did Savastano [a highly placed political figure] tell you that Ugo Montagna had a record, and that he was an ex-member of OVRA [Mussolini's secret police], and that at one time he acted as a pimp for the members of the Fascist Regime?" "Savastano didn't speak to me about Montagna's past," Caglio replies coolly. "He described Montagna as a good, loyal person who would be able to help me in my theatrical career." During testimony, lawyers ask Caglio what first prompted her to contact Silvano Muto after reading the article on Wilma Montesi in *Actuality*. "Certain aspects of an unidentified man reminded me of Ugo Montagna," Caglio responds. "The character described seemed like his: A man who gets everything he wants from women, who tells them not to smoke too much because it would be bad for them, and various other things."

According to Caglio, about a month after Montesi's death, Montagna acquires an apartment for Piero Piccioni's friend Tommaso Pavone, the chief of police. In exchange, Pavone promises to exercise the old Fascist "Writ of Obligatory Deportation" to rid Montagna of unwanted tenants in his various properties. Later, it will turn out that another individual with Pavone's name happens to live on a particular street where Montagna's concern had some dealings. In all likelihood, Caglio made a connection simply by looking up "Pavone" in the phone book. Real police chiefs, on the other hand, generally maintain unlisted numbers. The friendship between the two men apparently originated during the days when Montagna hid Pavone from German authorities who were seeking his arrest. Pavone had been a member of the Fascist Party, but, like so many, he turned "patriotic." In fact, he was arrested by Neo-Fascists and handed over to the Germans after trying to hide in Florence. Pavone was even incarcerated in Regina Coeli, but was released after two days because he felt ill.

We could film a scene in which Pavone toasts a young woman in evening dress with champagne. A paparazzo comes from nowhere, catches the two off guard, and snaps a photograph, shouting "Gotcha!" He rushes off to sell the picture to a left-wing paper, as Pavone calls after him, "Wait! She's my wife! It's New Year's Eve! Can't we have a glass of champagne?"

Scene in which Pavone submits his resignation from the national police force. Outside, officers rush around the city tearing down over sixteen thousand copies of Colonel Pompei's report on Ugo Montagna that have been plastered in public places. It is feared that crowds will form to read the posters up close, menacing public safety and the flow of traffic. The posters confirm that Montagna is a pimp, a spy, and a criminal.

Scene of a journalist speaking with friends and insisting that Pavone should be acquitted of all suspicion in the Montesi case because he has proven himself a true Italian by his service during the war.

All the facts contained in these notes for an unrealized screenplay were scrupulously researched. Whenever the author quotes dialogue, the words are taken verbatim from newspapers, magazines, or other journalistic accounts and trial transcripts. There are absolutely no inventions on the part of the author with regard to characters, plot, or dialogue. The following is not an exhaustive bibliography of all the materials that went into the preparation of this work, but rather a selection.

The primary journalistic sources for this book were the daily newspapers *Corriere della sera*, *Il messaggero di Roma*, *La stampa*, *Il giornale d'Italia*; and the magazines *L'europeo*, *Oggi*, and *Tempo*. Two important sources for photographs, gossip, and commentary on films and stars of the period are *Continental Film Review* and *Cinema nuovo*.

A number of books or book chapters directly related to the case provided secondary help:

Davis, Melton, S. *All Rome Trembled*. New York: Putnam, 1957. Nonfiction account of the case published just after the end of the Venice trial; lacking in broader perspective.

Del Duca, Natalino. *Documenta Zeta*. Rome: Tipografia Laboremus, 1955. Account of case by fortune teller with a grudge against Piero Piccioni. Suggests that Wilma was killed as she struggled to free herself from Piero's sexual advances. Her undergarments were burned in the police department furnace.

Enzensberger, Hans Magnus. "Wilma Montesi: Una vita dopo la morte" ["Wilma Montesi: Ein Leben nach dem Tode" (1969)], in *Politica e gangsterismo: Quattro saggi su criminalità comune e strutture di potere dalla Chicago degli anni '20 alla Roma degli anni '50*. Rome: Savelli, 1979. This essay notes that Italian justice differs from German justice in one fundamental aspect: whereas in Germany the criminal is simply construed by the public as Other, in Italy the criminal is no different from anyone else. In the case of Wilma Montesi, then, it was not enough for Italians to accept the girl's death as a fact of everyday life; instead, everyone had their say, and the investigation became a form of total self-investigation of the entire society. This, ultimately, is what our film should convey through some vast panoramic sweeps of Italy cities and towns, where everyone is talking about the Montesi scandal, if budgetary conditions were to allow for such scenes.

Galli, Giorgio. *Affari di stato*. Milan: Kaos Edizioni, 1991. This insightful book includes a chapter that places the Montesi scandal in the context of the "swindler's law" and other political moves of the period.

Gemma, Giuseppe. *Il mistero di Tor Vaianica*. Rome: Editrice arti grafiche Gemma, 1954. Self-published account produced during period of second investigation for inquiring Italian minds.

Kennet, Wayland. *The Montesi Scandal*. London: Faber and Faber, 1957. Written just after Venice trial by British author. "Those silly Italians with their daft politics." Lists all the funny names of the case's protagonists translated into English.

Márquez, Gabriel García. *Obra Periodistica*, vol. 4 (1955–1960), ed. Jacques Gilard. Barcelona: Brughera, 1983. Márquez was in Rome as a foreign correspondent and wrote about the case for a brief period. His articles are pithy, eloquent, poetic.

Montanelli, Indro. *Addio, Wanda! Rapporto Kinsey sulla situazione italiana*. Milan: Leo Longanesi, 1956. Strange account of fictitious Italian visit by Kinsey at behest of U.S. ambassador Clare Booth Luce. Kinsey diagnoses drop in Italian libido and critiques the Left.

Pellegrini, Rinaldo. *Il caso Montesi*. Parma: Ugo Guanda, 1954. Report by forensic pathologist hired to review case by Silvano Muto's lawyers. Concludes that criminal act did take place. Writes with "objectivity of Julian Benda's intellectual."

Scelba, Mario. *Per 1'Italia e per 1'Europa*. Rome: Edizioni Cinque Lune, 1990. Secretary of the Interior at the time of Wilma's death; later, prime minister during the investigative phase, Scelba writes briefly about the case in this memoir.

A number of books, articles, and other sources not directly related to the case provided inspiration:

Adinolfi, Francesco. *Mondo exotica: Suoni, visioni, manie della generazione cocktail*. Turin: Einaudi, 2000. Several chapters of this essential book treat the environment of the dolce vita nightclubs.

Bobbio, Norberto. *Left and Right: The Significance of a Political Distinction*. Translated by Allan Cameron. Chicago: University of Chicago Press, 1996.

Borgna, Gianni. *L'Italia di Sanremo*. Milan: Mondadori, 1998. Decades of pop music and middlebrow taste.

Cerami, Vincenzo. *Fattacci: Racconto di quattro delitti italiani*. Turin: Einaudi, 1997. Four "typically Italian" crimes. In one of these "ugly stories," Cerami provides a description of a victim as "borghesuccia"—"with a bit of a chest, wide thighs, an alert gaze, and strong ankles." This could be said to fit Wilma well.

Certeau, Michel de. *The Practice of Everyday Life*. Translated by Steven Rendall. Berkeley and Los Angeles: University of California Press, 1984.

Clément, Catherine. *Syncope: The Philosophy of Rapture*. Translated by Sally O'Driscoll and Deirdre M. Mahoney. Minneapolis: University of Minnesota Press, 1994.

Cohen, Margaret, and Christopher Prendergast, eds. *Spectacles of Realism: Body, Gender, Genre*. Minneapolis: University of Minnesota Press, 1995.

Flaiano, Ennio. *The Via Veneto Papers* [*La solitudine del satiro*]. Translated by John Satriano. Vermont: Marlboro Press, 1992. Diary of the writer's experiences making *La dolce vita* and hanging out on "the Street."

Garber, Marjorie, and Rebecca Walkowitz, eds. *Secret Agents: The Rosenberg Case, McCarthyism, and Fifties America*. New York and London: Routledge, 1995. Some of the essays in this volume are helpful for putting the struggle of the "democratic" and "sociocommunist" parties in Italy into a contextual relationship with McCarthyism, Hollywood, and American politics.

Handley, Susannah. *Nylon: The Story of a Fashion Revolution*. Baltimore: Johns Hopkins University Press, 1999. History of artificial fibers that may help to situate Wilma's garter belt in a larger cultural context.

Insolera, Italo. *Roma moderna: Un secolo di storia urbanistica: 1870–1970*. Turin: Einaudi, 1976. Corruption and missed opportunities in building and urban development.

Kaplan, Alice, and Kristin Ross, eds. *Yale French Studies: Everyday Life 73*. New Haven, Conn.: Yale University Press, 1987.

Kirby, Lynne, *Parallel Tracks: The Railroad and Silent Cinema*. Durham, N.C.: Duke University Press, 1997. An account of the profound links between "actuality," cinema at its origins, and trains.

Kracauer, Siegfried. *Theory of Cinema: The Redemption of Physical Reality*. Oxford: Oxford University Press, 1960.

Lefebvre, Henri. *Everyday Life in the Modern World*. Translated by Sacha Rabinovitch. New Brunswick, N.J.: Transaction Publishers, 1994.

———. *The Production of Space*. Translated by Donald Nicholson-Smith. Oxford: Basil Blackwell, 1991.

Moravia, Alberto. *La noia* [*Boredom*]. Milan: Bompiani, 1960. For a sense of the atmosphere in Rome of this period, this novel is required reading.

Murray, Timothy. *Like a Film: Ideological Fantasy on Screen, Camera, and Canvas*. London and New York: Routledge, 1993.

Ross, Kristin. *Fast Cars, Clean Bodies: Decolonization and the Reordering of French Culture*. Cambridge: MIT Press, 1995.

Setta, Sandro. *L'uomo qualunque*. Rome and Bari: Laterza, 1975. Account of immediate postwar politics and the rise of the "Anyman" Party.

Walsh, John. *Poe the Detective: The Curious Circumstances Behind the Mystery of Marie Roget*. New Brunswick, N.J.: Rutgers University Press, 1968. Account of actual case (Mary Rogers) on which Poe based the second of his Dupin tales. An apparently innocent girl disappears. Her body is found on the New Jersey side of the Hudson. Newspapers and detectives collaborate unconsciously to spread rumors. A year after Rogers's death, an innkeeper confesses to giving her a botched abortion. Poe is angry because this new closure would harm his (and Dupin's) reputation as a detective. Many parallels to the Montesi case.

Wu Ming. *54*. Turin: Einaudi, 2002. This wonderful historical-fictive novel, written by a collective that publishes under the Chinese term for "anonymous," came out after the present work had been largely completed. It must, however, be mentioned here, as several Bolognese in a bar offer their theories on the Montesi case, which served, in fact, as the very origin of the broader project.

Works on paparazzo photography and tabloidism of general interest:

Blessing, Jennifer. "Paparazzi on the Prowl." Pp. 324–334 in *The Italian Metamorphosis, 1943–1968*. Rome: Progetti Museali Editore, 1994.

Boas, Gary Lee. *Starstruck: Photographs from a Fan*. Los Angeles: Dilettante Press, 1999.

Koestenbaum, Wayne. "Shooting Stars." *Artforum International* 36 (November 1997): 9–10.

Mormorio, Diego. *Tazio Secchiaroli: Greatest of the Paparazzi*. Translated by Alexandra Bonfante-Warren. New York: Abrams, 1999.

Paparazzi: Fotografie di Velio Cioni, Marcello Geppetti, Tazio Secchiaroli, Elio Sorci, Sergio Spinelli. Edited by Paolo Costantini et al. Florence: Alinari, 1988. Catalogue of exhibit held at Palazzo Fortuny (Venice, 1988) details work of key group of paparazzi.

Photographs of Ron Galella, 1960–1990. Edited by Steven Bluttal. Los Angeles: Grey Bull Press, 2002. The paparazzo famous for stalking Jacqueline Onassis.

Quinn, Edward. *A Côte d'Azur Album*. Edited by Martin Heller. Zurich: Scalo Books, 1994.

———. *Stars, Stars, Stars: Off the Screen*. Zurich: Scalo Books, 1997.

Sante, Luc. *Evidence*. New York: Noonday Press, 1992. On crime scene photography.

Sekula, Alan. "Paparazzo Notes," from *Photography Against the Grain: Essays and Photo Works, 1973–1983*. Nova Scotia: The Press of the Nova Scotia College of Art and Design, 1984. Essential reading on Ron Galella.

Discography of Piero Piccioni (in art, Piero Morgan). A talented composer and film scorer. His filmography is too extensive to list here in its entirety, so we will limit ourselves to those titles that, ironically, would seem to have some connection to the scandal.

The Beach [La spiaggia] (1954, directed by Alberto Lattuada). This wonderful and underrated film, based on a short novel by Cesare Pavese, caused a scandal whose concentric ripples overlap with the Montesi case. The film suggests that the postwar bourgeoisie, in its drive to maintain wealth and privilege, openly tolerate corruption. Because the film's plot includes the suggestion of a nude bath on a beach in the Italian Riviera, the public made a connection with Wilma Montesi. We can take this as a prime example of the confusion between the inside and the outside of films.

Piccioni's first film score after the Venice trial was Summer Tales *(1958). This was followed by (among many others):*

From a Roman Balcony (1961)

The Assassin [L'assassino] (1961)

The City Prisoner [La città prigioniera] (1962)

Hands on the City [Le mani sulla città] (1963). This film, directed by Francesco Rosi, speaks openly about corruption in construction contracts.

The Moment of Truth [Il momento della verità] (1965)

The Tenth Victim [La decima vittima] (1965). "Futuristic Italian jazz" at its best.

I Knew Her Well [Io la conoscevo bene] (1966)

The Mattei Affair [Il caso Mattei] (1972). This film is included here not so much for the title (which does resound of the caso Montesi), but because it is about Enrico Mattei, a man who had an enormous influence on Italian politics, and who helped to modernize the press. Mattei died in 1962 in a suspicious plane explosion. An incredible film about conspiracy, lies, and politics.

Excellent Cadavers [Cadaveri eccellenti] (1976)

Death Vengeance (1982)

I Know That You Know That I Know [Io so che tu sai che lo so] (1982)

Chronicle of a Death Foretold (1987)

Absolved for Having Committed the Crime [Assolto per aver commesso il fatto] (1992). This title nearly perfectly mirrors Piccioni's sentence in our own screenplay, with the addition of a simple negation.

Easy Tempo Vols. 1, 2, 3, released in 1996 by Right Tempo Classics in Italy. Includes various tracks by Piccioni and by Armando Trovaioli.

Beat Records has an extensive catalog of soundtracks, some from erotic Italian films of the 1960s and 1970s, including various tracks by Piccioni and Trovaioli.

An excellent record by an indie rock band that has declared a debt to Piero Piccioni is The High Llamas, *Cold and Bouncy* (V2, 1998).

We *might choose to use some of these tracks for our own film, although it is unlikely we would be granted the rights.*

◯

The viewer will note that these outtakes to the unrealized film on the Montesi scandal do not offer a solution to the case. They leave open multiple possibilities, and point the viewer to other sources. Should an unexpected deathbed confession lend closure to the scandal, we would certainly include it—or a respectable simulation—in the director's cut.

PHOTO CREDITS

Pages xi, 21, 34, 37, 123: Film stills from *La Dolce Vita*, 1960, Federico Fellini. Courtesy Museum of Modern Art, New York, Film Stills Archive.

Pages 5 (upper left, upper right), 27 (left and right), 47, 56–58, 60–61, 75, 79, 98, 100, 112, 118, 122: Photos from *L'europeo*, courtesy Domus Editorial Group.

Pages 5 (lower left), 24: Photos from *Oggi* magazine.

Page 5 (lower right): Photograph by Franco Pinna. © Archivio Tazio Secchiaroli/David Secchiaroli.

Page 7: Film still from *The Golden Coach*, 1952, Jean Renoir. Courtesy Museum of Modern Art, New York, Film Stills Archive.

Pages 11, 18–19: Film stills from *The Bicycle Thief*, 1948, Vittorio De Sica. Courtesy Museum of Modern Art, New York, Film Stills Archive.

Pages 15, 45, 77: Film stills from *Love in the City*, 1953. Courtesy Museum of Modern Art, New York, Film Stills Archive.

Pages 30, 67, 71, 89, 110: Courtesy Olympia Publifoto, Milan.

Pages 49, 82–83: © Archivio Tazio Secchiaroli/David Secchiaroli.

Page 52: Film still from *Funny Face*, 1957, Stanley Donen. Courtesy Museum of Modern Art, New York, Film Stills Archive.

Page 87: Photo by Velio Cioni. © Archivio Tazio Secchiaroli/David Secchiaroli.

Page 114: Film still from *The Paradine Case*, 1947, Alfred Hitchcock. Courtesy Museum of Modern Art, New York, Film Stills Archive.

Page 120: Courtesy of Velio Cioni.